Complete Cloud Compliance

How regulated industries de-risk
the cloud and kickstart transformation

Travis Good, MD & Kris Gösser

Printed in the United States of America. Published by Blurb, Inc.

Second Edition, November 2018.

Cover design by Ryan Tait. Art direction by Milepost59. Book design & production by R. Allan White.

Disclaimer: This book gives advice on how to manage compliance on the cloud. Although the authors and publisher have made every effort to ensure that the information in this book was correct at press time, the authors and publisher do not assume and hereby disclaim any liability to any party for any loss, damage, or disruption caused by errors or omissions, whether such errors or omissions result from negligence, accident, or any other cause.

Table of Contents

Cloud Compliance is Worth the Investment

By Hector Rodriguez,
Worldwide Health Chief Information Security Officer,
Microsoft

Not that long ago, many businesses and organizations viewed security and privacy compliance as a perfunctory expense. It was to be managed by a handful of employees as efficiently as possible, a lot like maintaining buildings or vehicle fleets.

Today, with cyberattacks and data breaches occurring daily, and the introduction of stricter regulatory requirements like Europe's General Data Protection Regulation (GDPR), compliance can no longer be an afterthought. It's an essential investment in the business, and a responsibility shared by all.

The growth of cloud computing has only raised the stakes. More and more customer information and business systems are hosted at data centers, which are often owned by third parties that may even be located in another country. Compliance has never been more complex. But that's exactly why it's so valuable.

Having strong privacy and security requirements in place can help a business build trust with customers, who need to know that their sensitive business data will be protected. It's a potential differentiator that can help win and sustain business.

An effective compliance program enables the rest of the company, and its customers, to focus more on building and running a great business. I see this regularly in my job working with healthcare companies, which must meet strict regulatory requirements. Their job is providing great medical care, not overseeing their vendors' or partners' compliance efforts.

That doesn't mean that they don't have a role to play in compliance. Some sharing of responsibility takes place, and it's important for everyone to understand their contribution. In fact, the responsibility matrix now extends well beyond the executive suite and the chief technology officer or the chief information officer.

Many companies today employ a chief privacy officer who works with the compliance staff and information security professionals to craft and govern the compliance strategy. In healthcare, every participant in the storage, transmission, processing or analysis of information in the cloud needs to understand that they are handling highly sensitive data.

Understanding the rules and being able to implement them during design, development, and testing stages makes it easier to operationalize compliance once you're in production and all the way through aftermarket support. In general, an effective compliance program should include the following:

- Company-wide privacy and security policy
- Access controls
- Identity management system
- Threat monitoring program
- Data governance and protection framework

It's important for executives to stand behind the company's policy and to urge the entire company to adhere to it. The leadership team must make it clear that they follow the policies and strategies themselves.

To create a culture that embraces compliance requires education and training. As an example, at Microsoft, we require every single employee to take formal ethics and compliance training each year.

Companies that are out of compliance usually have a culture that begins with the executives and the frontline managers and then permeates to the day-to-day workers. If people say that noncompliance is allowed, then that's what they do.

That's no longer an acceptable approach – if it ever was. Today, machines can recognize our faces and understand our speech, even to the point where they can guess our age or whether we have a cold. And we're just beginning to see what data-driven companies can do with all of the data that's now in the cloud.

A formal, comprehensive approach to compliance will help reduce a company's business and legal risks and keep customers happy. Compliance needs to be a common thread that appears in everything we do. It is not a distraction, but a central part of the business. It's well worth the investment.

Overcoming the Barriers of Compliance

This book is a new take on mitigating one of the greatest barriers to business innovation and transformation: compliance from heavy-handed regulations. We believe cloud adoption is crucial for businesses to remain relevant. We also believe that within regulated industries the burden of compliance blocks innovation necessary to compete in the future.

This book makes sense out of the apparent ambiguity among compliance and the cloud.

We believe one cause is education. Technologists have a debilitating misunderstanding about the concept of compliance. Lawyers and compliance officers struggle to keep up with the blistering pace of technology turnover. Combined, both sides fail to see how the modern cloud fits into the roadmap of a regulated company.

Our pedagogy is straightforward: We go deep on compliance in a way most engineering professionals can understand, then do the same deep exploration on the cloud in a way that a business-orientated compliance officer can comprehend. After that, we follow up with a thorough recommendation on how a newly marshaled team can collaboratively grapple compliance to enable a cloud-based technology strategy.

This is a book focused on healthcare's greatest challenge...

It is written for healthcare decision makers, large and small, primarily within the U.S. healthcare system, that any organization that handles protected health information will discover an essential new way of thinking about the problem of compliance.

New digital health startups will find the information we provide invaluable as they build their compliance strategies. Many will be disappointed to learn that the burden of compliance is table stakes for doing business, but it's the truth. We aim to quickly educate you and get you on a path towards growth.

Most likely, larger healthcare enterprises will find the core of the *Complete Cloud Compliance* program to be a missing piece for business transformation strategies. If that's you, this book will guide you on your journey.

...But best practices are best practices

Throughout the book, you will hear, *best practices are best practices.* When envisioning a program by which conservative healthcare regimes could be managed on the modern cloud, we came to understand that the ideas behind *Complete Cloud Compliance* extend to any geography, across any compliance regime, in any industry.

We focus on healthcare because it is our expertise, but we believe this is essential reading for compliance officers in other regulated industries, like finance or education. Incidentally, all are mired in a fight for survival as cloud-native competitors out-flank their incumbent business models. The call to arms is as universal as the ideas presented in this book.

If you do not work in healthcare, we encourage you to expand the healthcare use cases woven throughout into your own domain. We are confident you will find value.

CHAPTER 1

The Business Case for Compliance

Regulated companies risk obsolescence when new technology isn't adopted fast enough. Likewise, legacy business models risk being marginalized by shifting customer expectations. Those shifts occur when digital experiences improve, combined with changing market conditions that spiral out of control. Even healthcare, the most regulated industry with the heartiest entrenchment and uniquely perverse economic incentives, is nearing a complete upheaval due to a litany of world-changing ideas, like mobile devices, Internet of Things, big data, and artificial intelligence. These innovations stem from the parent of all modern technology innovations, the cloud. Adoption of cloud computing remains the root challenge for new and existing companies in regulated industries, and compliance contributes to the lack thereof.

Stakes get higher while the pace gets faster

Societies adopt technology at the rate at which they can absorb the change brought on by that technology. Eventual assimilation requires a mix of economic, political, cultural, business, and technological factors. Some changes are easily absorbed by a society, like those found with mobile phones moving from 4G to LTE spectrums, while other changes like self-driving cars take decades.

The internet is tricky. On one hand, it is pervasive in the everyday lives of consumers and society in general has absorbed it fairly quickly. But on the other hand, it has proven to be one of the more difficult technologies for large institutions, and in particular enterprise businesses, to absorb because it touches nearly every facet of civilization. It has not only upended personal hobbies and industries but powerful governments and the global economy itself. The internet unraveled the publishing industry in the 1990s, and now, every industry is experiencing major disruption. The advent of the cloud in the mid-2000s is the primary reason.

The difference between disruption in 1994 when innovations like Netscape popularized the web, and disruption now, arises from the previously impossible cost, speed, reach, and resiliency benefits of the cloud. The age of the internet can be split into two eras: pre-cloud and post-cloud. The pre-cloud era, stretching from early 1990s to mid-2000s, reinforced incumbent institutional models. The post-cloud era, starting with the increased availability of Amazon Web Services (AWS) in 2006 and the introduction of the Apple iPhone in 2007, created conditions that have led to institutional upheaval felt across the planet. Over the last decade the result has been a rate of societal change unmatched in modern history.

That sounds dramatic, but it's true. Books of recorded facts and stories about this societal evolution could theoretically fill entire libraries, so this book won't attempt complete coverage of the impact. However, one must only look around to appreciate the point: everything is substantially different. Houses are now smart. Cars are incrementally autonomous. Communications with families are instantaneous and global (with periodic emojis included, changing human language as we know it). Mostly anyone can buy mostly anything, mostly anywhere. An interactive map of the entire world is pocketed for convenience. A substantial amount of all information known to humankind lies ready to be searched and found. In 1998, none of these changes existed in a useful state. Twenty years later, they are a regular reality.

This blistering pace of change enables some parts of society to absorb its benefits and ramifications better than others. Those who keep pace receive a competitive advantage with every new innovation, much like compounding bank interest, while those companies that don't keep pace lag further behind and remain in danger of disruption or, worse, obsolescence.

Lagging behind

One way to split those companies that can absorb the rapid pace of cloud-based innovation versus those that can't is through the lens of regulation. Highly-regulated industries struggle to incorporate modern web innovations that would spur the transformation required to compete in this new era of business models, while lightly-regulated industries move quickly, altering customer expectations rapidly.

Regulated industries are, by definition, risk-averse. For cloud-based technology, this risk aversion is rooted in the complexity of understanding where liabilities actually exist between the data center and the users of digital products. Outdated regulations haven't kept pace with the dynamic nature of the cloud, further accentuating a problem: compliance confusion.

Ultimately, regulations applied to the cloud boil down to security and privacy. In that light, complying with regulations on protecting data privacy sounds like it should be cut and dried. Governments set privacy rules and companies follow them. Those that don't are penalized. Extremely simple in concept.

Yet, compliance is squishier than that. Compliance needs to evolve and respond to ongoing changes in the market caused by technological innovation.

Compliance behaves like a lagging indicator to technology because it proceeds from regulation. By definition, regulation is meant to police something that already exists. The evolution of compliance has tracked with the evolution of how regulated industries can absorb technological innovations. In many ways compliance is like the final ink drying on the paper to explain how the world understands and has absorbed a certain type of macro technology. Compliance follows innovation, it doesn't predict or predate it. Compliance is a reactive thing, and businesses should refrain from the associated realities.

The business case for compliance hinges on an organization's ability to minimize security and privacy risks in a dynamic cloud-based world that changes monthly. Business organizations need to keep up. However, the conditions that go into this challenge are so complex that most organizations don't know where to start.

Compliance vs innovation

The previous discussion lays out the tension that exists between compliance management programs and technological innovations that drive business transformation.

Even the most conservative industries, like healthcare and finance, understand the warning: innovate or die. Fortunately, the cloud accelerates transformation more than any other technology paradigm. So, the correlated warning should be: adopt the cloud or be disrupted by those that do. One need only look at Netflix's displacement of Blockbuster, Uber's impact on transportation, and social media's effect on entire governments to understand that most major consumer experiences today have been touched by the cloud.

That level of innovation—where entirely new business models make incumbents obsolete—largely happens outside of regulated industries. Healthcare and finance haven't seen as much disruption to date, but it's coming. End-user technologies like mobile devices and artificial intelligence are being adopted across global communities, thus changing the experience expectations of customers. Businesses in regulated industries are not immune to similar disruption, however, while they devise a plan to prevent inevitable death. Uncertainty remains in knowing the right way to facilitate cloud-based innovation while meeting the regulatory frameworks across multiple geographies.

Deep within the boardrooms of highly-regulated companies, the risk calculus has surprisingly not yet flipped. Even in 2018, many executives and board members view cloud-based business transformation as a riskier use of strategic initiatives than sticking with the status quo. While everyone accepts and acknowledges the need to innovate via the cloud, compliance and other drivers have essentially blocked adoption of innovation practices due to fear of new innovations being non-compliant.

Owing to the inevitable systemic disruption brought by the cloud, this calculus is a fundamental and existential risk to organizations. The grand ultimatum is proving true: adopt, or eventually be disrupted.

Education can change the current calculus, by breaking down complex topics into digestible ideas. Arming **compliance decision makers** with solid technology knowledge surrounding the modern cloud, and equipping **technology decision makers** with a greater understanding of how compliance works is the first step.

CHAPTER 2

What *Really* is Compliance?

Protecting data is the highest priority of any digital technology. Hacking someone's personal information, whether originating from a Russian criminal organization or a celebrity-spotting Beverly Hills nurse, is a serious matter. All industries remain on watch for such hacking, and every organization has much to lose. The global nature of digital technology and digital data opens up organizations to significant risk, related to both regulatory compliance regimes across multiple geographies and damage to invaluable reputations. When organizations understand compliance, they comprehend its meaningful business implications. This chapter will cover compliance generally and healthcare as a specific use case.

A primer: the roles of privacy, security, and compliance

Three distinct functions have emerged to help protect organizational assets, data, and reputation: privacy, security, and compliance. All three functions are commonly misunderstood, especially the interplay between them. Before delving into the depths of compliance and the cloud, it is essential to clarify the definitions of privacy, security, and compliance and how they relate to each other.

Privacy. As a distinct function, privacy is the newest of the three for most organizations. Privacy's role for an organization is to define and evangelize the standards and rules for the right of individuals to be left alone, be a champion for data privacy, both internally and externally, and ensure the organizational handling of data aligns with both the internal mission and values of the organization as well as the external regulatory requirements. Privacy within an organization can reside within the compliance office, but often acts as an independent function. To demonstrate privacy's uniqueness, consider that the Health Insurance Portability and Accountability Act (HIPAA) mandates that organizations appoint a Privacy Officer in charge of this responsibility; HIPAA also contains two broad sections – the Privacy Rule and the Security Rule.

Security. In its simplest form, security implements controls to prevent unauthorized access to organizational systems and data; these can be both physical and logical controls. Security commonly pulls from the CIA information security triad of confidentiality, integrity, and availability of data to inform its role in an organization. As a function, it is in charge of executing and maintaining an organization's information security program. This is the most easily understood function of the three and the most clearly established at most organizations. Security often sits within an organization's IT group.

Compliance. Briefly, compliance ensures the privacy standards and security program are in place and meet a required set of rules or laws. Traditionally, compliance has simply been a snapshot of an organization's security posture. As the pace of technology, and the cloud, has accelerated, so too has the need for compliance to function in a more continual fashion versus a snapshot. Compliance often does, and should, sit outside of IT and security groups, as its role is to assess the information security program.

Readers will find this book places heavy emphasis on cloud-based compliance. The transformational shift generated by the cloud is only successfully enabled if security and privacy also shift in their fundamental approaches with compliance. An organization's privacy, security, and compliance programs must be synchronized to successfully digitally transform and adopt the cloud.

Often, being compliant is seen as the outcome of a successful information security program, i.e., if you do everything right with security, then compliance is almost automatic. Make no mistake: this is akin to the tail wagging the dog. This book takes a different view, one shaped from years of privacy, security, and compliance on the cloud experience.

Compliance, along with privacy, should be a partner function to security that monitors the information security program at an organization. Policies should be created that inform the actual processes and implementations of security controls, which should be continually monitored to ensure compliance in real time, not as a snapshot. When compliance is not engaged and "sold" on new technology and platforms, like the cloud, organizations will not be able to fully adopt them. Compliance should be a program unto itself and not an after-thought from security engineers.

In practical terms, these functions should operate hand-in-hand with a very tight feedback loop. Organizations should push to eliminate internal politics to make this collaboration a reality.

How compliance works

To use compliance as an asset and an enabler of cloud-based transformation for an organization, one must first understand the building blocks.

Compliance has six distinct, but related components.

Standards Developing Organizations (SDO). An SDO or "standards body" sets definitions adopted by industry participants within a certain geography. Sometimes these organizations are international, like the International Organization for Standards (ISO) or the International Electronic Commission (IEC). Some organizations are national, like the American Institute of Certified Public Accountants (AICPA) or the National Institute of Standards and Technology (NIST). Some are industry-driven, like the HITRUST Alliance and the Payment Card Industry Security Standards Council (PCI). Often organizations collaborate, like when the ISO and the IEC combined to define a set of corporate governance standards or HITRUST and the AICPA to normal-ize compliance requirements. Almost always these organizations set standards adopted by regulations and frameworks.

Standards. How long is a meter? How many hours are in a day? How many bits is your encryption at rest? Standards are fundamental to efficient human collaboration, with documentation and societal influence going back millen-nia. In the world of technology compliance, standards are set nationally and internationally by governments and independent organizations. ISO and NIST publish the most commonly known standards in this area, with ISO/IEC 27001 as a frequent example.

Regulations. Quite often, government regulations are mistakenly interpreted by those new to this space as direct replacements for the concept of compliance. Regulations are not compliance but instead contribute to a larger concept of compliance by creating the rules which compliance programs must adhere. HIPAA is a well-known example in the United States. Regulations come with penalties attached. Those penalties become the primary focus of businesses with an internal compliance management program.

Rules. The output from regulations are rules. A set of rules are the specific directions regulated companies must follow. Rules are often ambiguous and non-prescriptive. More important to the world of technology, they often don't keep up with the rate of change, meaning interpretation of how to adhere to a rule might dramatically change year-over-year.

Frameworks. The world of standards and regulations across multiple industries and geographies can be dizzying, which is why frameworks exist. Frameworks are a tool, typically published by organizations or independent bodies, to manage or control for specific regulatory rules. HITRUST's CSF within United States healthcare and COBIT internationally for IT governance are two common examples.

Controls. The output from frameworks are controls. A framework will have a catalog of controls, all mapped to specific rules. A control is purposefully prescriptive, defining how someone would implement a procedure to account for a given rule. Therefore, a regulated company would ultimately strive to meet a certain collection of controls in order to demonstrate their compliance of a specific regulation. For example, someone who implements a certain number of HITRUST CSF controls can go through an assessment process to then claim HIPAA compliance.

Standards Developing Organizations	→ Standards	*e.g. ISO outputs ISO 27001*
Regulations	→ Rules	*e.g. HIPAA outputs Rule § 164.312*
Frameworks	→ Controls	*e.g. HITRUST CSF outputs Control 12.d*

Compliance is the interplay of these six components resulting in a business, organization, or individual demonstrating verification that they have successfully met the rules of an organization. This is what "compliance" means.

Going global

While HIPAA is a famous American regulation, the challenge of compliance on the cloud is global. New global business models spurred by cloud adoption also refer to the digital connections across countries and continents. More than ever, digital businesses operate in a global market, which means the more restrictive policies do cross international borders. Let's break it down.

Some SDOs are national, like NIST in the United States, while some are international, like ISO, but due to the global nature of compliance, national ones like NIST are increasingly receiving broad acceptance internationally. Both perform the same function—setting standards and guidelines—but where and how the output from these organizations is applied can vary based on geography. For example, the standards set by NIST are not immediately applicable in Australia, but the Australian Cyber Security Centre (ACSC) tapped work put forth by ISO/IEC when creating its Information Security Registered Assessors Program (IRAP). The standards which come from these organizations are thusly national while pulling from international inspiration. In many ways, the global nature of an organization is an advantage since its standards can lend more of a "one-and-done" approach.

Most regulations are inherently national because they come from a governing authority. As an example, HIPAA does not inherently apply outside the United States. However, regulations are increasingly crossing borders. Taking HIPAA as an example, Covered Entities can be global while many digitally-based Business Associates are increasingly located international as well. A simple example is the use of data centers in Asia.

One of the best examples can be found in Europe with the General Data Protection Regulation (GDPR). This much-anticipated new European Union security and privacy regime went into effect on May 25, 2018. GDPR leaves some discretion to EU member states, but, as a general rule, applies to any company dealing with the personal data of EU citizens.

GDPR sets clear guidelines that strictly protect the privacy of individuals across industries, with some distinctions. For example, within healthcare, GDPR explicitly applies to physical and mental health data, genetic data, and biometric data. That data can only be accessed (1) with specific consent from the individual, (2) for health and social care, or (3) for public health (such as cross-border containment of an infectious disease).

Strict requirements also exist for reporting a security breach within 72 hours from becoming aware of it. In the United States, any organization would have breach reporting timelines in its policies and contracts, but most breach reporting timelines stipulated by major cloud providers and vendors are much longer: days, weeks, or even months.

Some of the more challenging components of GDPR are centered on the rights of individuals to obtain access to all of their data or the right to be forgotten, meaning the right to have all personally identifiable information (PII) data deleted. The complexity of this specific regulation cannot be understated since the specialty of PII per respective industry changes how and where data is managed. Granting access to all personal health data or being able to delete all health data is a high bar to meet, especially for large, bloated electronic health records and legacy healthcare software.

One important contribution of GDPR is the overarching principle of data protection by design and default. Sadly, security and compliance are often an afterthought at best or perceived as an unnecessary box to check at worst. GDPR explicitly attempts to resolve this pattern by anchoring risk assessment, analysis, and management to the entire lifecycle of products and services to ensure data is protected and secure.

GDPR doesn't mess around. Penalties for violations can be as high as 20 million euros or 4% of global revenue, whichever is greater. Given the practicality of the regulation, legal precedent can only be determined with ensuing years. Legal interpretation turns GDPR from a physical European liability to a conceptually global one. Ironically, global regulations like GDPR, as opposed to global organizations and standards, pose more liability threat considering more permutations of risk exist.

So why does such a burdensome compliance regime even stand?

GDPR is a direct result of frustration by the European Union (EU) with Google, and other companies like Google, that over the past ten years have had multi-billion dollar antitrust style lawsuits from the EU because European culture doesn't tolerate private companies having so much insight and data on its citizens, and that Europeans don't have any control. Generally speaking, the EU and its citizens believe government has a duty to protect and control this data.

When Google played hardball, the EU updated the Data Protection Directive, a 1995 regulation that more explicitly protects the rights of its citizens in today's internet age. In no way is GDPR proactive; it is reactive regulation.

With some irony, compliance and regulation have only helped cement the incumbents and the monopoly. It's no wonder that technology titans like Mark Zuckerberg, Facebook's founder and CEO, say "Yes please, regulate me." Zuckerberg understands that if regulators say organizations can't let data in or out of the house, the organizations that have all the data win.

Compliance can also be considered mushy since it can't be viewed as black or white. Decisions about compliance are not necessarily binary, technical questions that can be clearly measured. The final stage of compliance is a matter of legal precedent, which for GDPR none yet exist.

With a fine that can reach four percent of global revenue, no organization wants to be the first to set that legal precedent. How will fines be enforced? How are bad actors identified? The risk of not complying is too great, so business organizations will comply.

The challenge posed from managing the variability, combined with the global nature of compliance is one of this book's central themes. A cloud-based business operating in a global economy is inherently required to deploy a global compliance management program.

WHAT'S A "COMPLIANCE REGIME"?

A regime is the collective approach by a business to use standards and frameworks to manage the risks and liabilities associated to a given regulation. Liable organizations should have a plan to manage the regimes of HIPAA or GDPR, for example.

Globally Applicable

CSA STAR
ISO/IEC 20000-1
ISO/IEC 22301
ISO/IEC 27001
ISO/IEC 27017
ISO/IEC 27018
SOC 1/2/3 Type 2
PCI DSS

Canada

PIPEDA
PIPA
BC FIPPA

U.S.

CJIS
DFARS
DoD DISA
FedRAMP
FIPS 140-2
HIPAA
HITRUST
MARS-E
GLBA
FERPA
GxP
Shared Assessments
SOX
FFIEC
ITAR

Argentina

PDPA

New Zealand

Government CC Framework

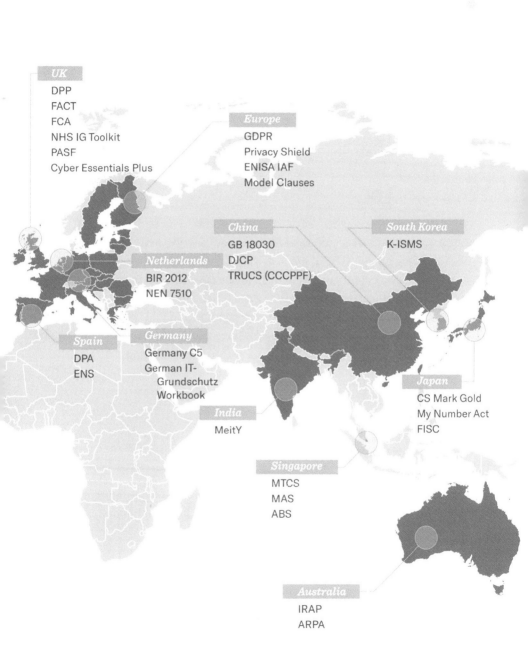

UK
DPP
FACT
FCA
NHS IG Toolkit
PASF
Cyber Essentials Plus

Europe
GDPR
Privacy Shield
ENISA IAF
Model Clauses

China
GB 18030
DJCP
TRUCS (CCCPPF)

South Korea
K-ISMS

Netherlands
BIR 2012
NEN 7510

Spain
DPA
ENS

Germany
Germany C5
German IT-Grundschutz Workbook

India
MeitY

Japan
CS Mark Gold
My Number Act
FISC

Singapore
MTCS
MAS
ABS

Australia
IRAP
ARPA

How HIPAA works: An illustrative compliance use case

Portability and accountability are the first-order principles that explains the purpose of HIPAA, a regulation requiring PHI handled by Covered Entities and their Business Associates is secure and patient privacy is respected.

Originally passed in 1996, HIPAA set out to modernize the workflow of health information. Even though paper-based at the time, the health data in medical records were on the march toward the digital age with the proliferation of desktop personal computer workstations. Now, all healthcare entities and organizations that use, store, maintain or transmit patient health information are expected to be in complete compliance with HIPAA regulations, which are designed to ensure privacy, reduce fraudulent activity, and improve data system processing. To the government's credit, its efforts to protect patients in a future digital world held tremendous foresight. Unfortunately, many of the regulations technologically lagged behind the moment they were signed into law because that future digital world did not anticipate concepts like the cloud.

The U.S. government continued to expand on HIPAA through additional installations. The Privacy Rule, which took effect in 2003, covers most of a patient's payment history and medical record, and focuses on a patient's right to restrict access to individually identifiable information. The Security Rule, which took effect in 2005, focuses on safeguards to protect the confidentiality and integrity of patient data. In 2009, the government passed the Health Information Technology for Economic and Clinical Health Act, or HITECH Act, which extended coverage of the rules while adding an additional one around breach notification enforcement. On January 2013, "the final ruling" combined everything, creating the HIPAA Final Omnibus, which consists of numerous standards and implementation specifications, some of which are required while others are addressable (but still mandatory), that cover who can access the data, how a patient can give consent to share data, and how to identify and authenticate users who are trying to access the data.

When organizations follow these rules in the United States, the healthcare industry commonly refers to that adherence as HIPAA compliance.

Here's how HIPAA works in practice. HIPAA uses the phrasing of a Covered Entity, Business Associate, and Subcontractor. HIPAA directly defines Covered Entities as providers (hospitals, clinics, etc), payers (insurance, etc.), and processors (clearing houses). A Business Associate is any other organization that provides services to a Covered Entity that creates or handles PHI. In the final 2013 ruling, government administrators applied an additional distinction: the Subcontractor, which is essentially a Business Associate of a Business Associate.

Compliance is where the rubber meets the road between, say, a hospital and a digital health technology company or a cloud service provider. That's why compliance isn't complete until a Business Associate Agreement (BAA) exists that outlines which aspects of the risk each organization is responsible for and which party is liable in a data breach incident.

A successful compliance story is when a Business Associate—the digital technology company or cloud service provider—understands the full scope of compliance and properly articulates the division of responsibilities to be assumed. This Business Associate has policies and procedures that are translated down to technology that is proven to address corresponding responsibilities. The Covered Entity—hospital, clinic, insurance company—is assured the Business Associate meets requirements and contractually agrees to work with them. Only then can the Covered Entity and the Business Associate focus on bringing technology and innovation into the system to improve the lives of patients.

Liability is then chained within BAAs cascading from Business Associates to Subcontractors. A Business Associate might work with one or more Subcontractors, each providing a specific service within the Business Associate's offering to the Covered Entity. If the Subcontractor is passed PHI from the Business Associate, then the Subcontractor must meet the same level of organizational HIPAA compliance as the Business Associate specific to the service outlined in the mutual Business Associate Agreement.

HIPAA
Violations
2004-2015

69%
of violations result in
corrective actions

Total Number of HIPAA Violations: **34,632**

Average HIPAA Violations Per Year: **2,886**

Average Number of Corrective Actions Taken: **1,982**

The penalties are real

Many different types of HIPAA violations abound, but in the world of patient-based software products, cloud or otherwise, a violation typically means when a security breach, or "breach incident," happens. To add insult to injury, when a breach incident does occur, HIPAA compliance requires the breachee to notify all entities for which it has a signed BAA of the incident within a certain period of time. What a wonderful example of the unintended complexity of compliance due to a lack of standardization. Hang in there on this: Because of non-standard BAAs, that could mean that the breachee (a Subcontractor that provides managed database services, we'll call them Party A) must notify a Business Associate (a SaaS product that sells to hospitals, we'll call them Party B) within 72 hours given the terms in their mutual BAA, but Party B's BAA with a Covered Entity (a hospital, we'll call them Party C) required Party B to notify Party C of a breach within four hours. How does Party B manage that? They don't, and Party A's negligence, along with Party B's poor BAA management, puts Party B in similar trouble as Party A in the first place. Ultimately, Party C, the Covered Entity in this case, is not notified in a timeline to meet its own compliance policies. It's a mess.

Covered Entity
e.g. Hospital or Health System

4 hour breach notification

Business Associate
e.g. Digital Health Application

72 hour breach notification

Subcontractor
e.g. Managed Database Vendor

That's one simple and amusing illustration of the compliance complexity.

Remember, though, fines aren't the only way to be penalized. Bad publicity, often feared more by large corporations than a simple fine, can send stock prices and public perception tumbling. In fact, the larger the corporation, the more chance bad publicity will negatively impact business compared to a fine levied by the U.S. government.

Navigating uncertainty

HIPAA isn't a law with clearly prescribed definitions of adherence, especially at the technology level. For example, HIPAA §164.312(a)(1) gives specifics around access control, with HIPAA §164.312(a)(2) giving two required and two addressable implementation guidelines. Essentially, HIPAA §164.312(a) says, You should limit access using these four types of implementations. What that means for implementation in 2003 compared to 2018 is dramatically different. As one can imagine, technology, especially in the cloud, has far outpaced the initial understandings of regulators in 1996, 2003, or even 2013.

Intense disagreement has arisen around what it means to be compliant, since absolute certainty of compliance is not possible. In U.S. healthcare, "HIPAA compliance" is nothing more than an interpretation of the HIPAA Omnibus Rule, ideally applied in a way that is both reasonable and appropriate to the overall risk profile of the organization and technology. Officers in charge of compliance at a vendor review all relationships and protocols, then offer legal opinions as to whether the vendor and its technology meet the intent of the HIPAA Omnibus. Those compliance officers in charge of compliance at a hospital may trust the vendor, but will still run their own audit, using a "trust but verify" approach. Disputes often arise as two lawyers argue over a given definition.

The Healthcare Compliance Association's *CHC Candidate Handbook: Detailed Content Outline*[1] , offers a guide to the elements of a compliance program:

- Standards, policies, and procedures
- Compliance program administration
- Screening and evaluation of employees, physicians, vendors and other agents
- Communication, education, and training on compliance issues
- Monitoring, auditing, and internal reporting systems
- Discipline for noncompliance
- Investigations and remedial measures

Yet even the field's leading experts take great pains to ensure compliance is not prescriptive. In January 2017, a group of compliance professionals and staff from the Department of Health and Human Services, Office of Inspector General met to discuss ways of measuring the effectiveness of compliance programs and developed a comprehensive list of potential metrics against each of these elements[2]. Still, the group cautioned against treating this as a checklist to be applied when assessing a compliance program, they further discouraged anyone to use this list as a standard or a certification due to difficulty with pinning down specifics.

How to map HIPAA controls amid rule uncertainty

Engineering teams find the legal ambiguity within government regulations to be a nuisance. Yet, understanding the vocabulary helps.

First, regulations have rules. Unfortunately, these rules are typically not prescriptive. Wherever the use of "rule" is used when explaining compliance, consider it an actual directive from a regulation, even if it is most often insufficient in its directions.

Second, how an organization manages itself against a rule is called a control. Catalogs of controls typically make up a framework.

Third, implementing a compliance maturity model against the controls is the best way to address the implementation or process of the control that is mapped to the rule.

A maturity model is a sliding scale that categorizes an organization's effectiveness at meeting the definition of a specific compliance control. The maturity model is applied directly to an individual control. When applied to HIPAA in this context, an organization would have a constellation of maturity model ratings across a scoped number of framework controls against the HIPAA Omnibus rules that apply to the organization.

Using the earlier analogy, applying a maturity model helps improve the processes and eventual effectiveness of preventing students running in the hall. A maturity model grades the implementation of controls to stop running, like hall monitors, cameras, or student education.

A Capability Maturity Model (CMM)[3] is the most common maturity model applied to various compliance regimes. Initially developed by the Department of Defense in the 1950s, different incarnations of a CMM have emerged throughout the decades. The structure is simple: create five maturity levels along a continuum; define the key practices that cause something to move from one level to another; and then normalize the definitions that apply to everything within a domain scope. Note that maturity model levels aren't applied to rules, but to controls.

The approach developed by Carnegie Mellon of "Strength, Breadth, Rigor"[4] has been the main model by which compliance has been managed. A simple summary of five maturity levels used by cloud-based organizations:

1. **Policy** — The organization has documented policies for a specific control, thus demonstrating the organization's understanding of the control. Without policies in place, the organization has no guarantee of understanding the control well enough to implement.

2. **Procedure** — The organization creates a process to implement a control. The process can be manual or automated, but the key in a cloud-based world centers on being documented and repeatable.

3. **Implemented** — The organization has implemented the process for the control. This is usually an acceptable level to reach in order to pass an audit.

4. **Measured** — The organization has a way by which to measure the effectiveness of the implemented control.

5. **Managed** — The organization takes continuous measurement of the implemented control and applies ongoing management of the control in order to refine its implementation to improve efficacy.

All combined, the job of a cloud-based organization is to map HIPAA rules to a control framework, then document how the organization will technically implement the control in a repeatable way, thus ensuring the control is properly measured for improvement. Viewed in that light, HIPAA compliance on the cloud isn't that scary.

What's great about the maturity model is how elegantly it maps to the roles of privacy, security, and compliance. The three roles fulfill a linear sequence when overlaid with the maturity model.

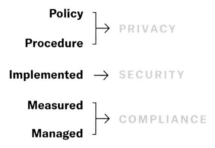

Privacy goes first. In many respects, privacy can be summarized as the role of defining how an organization will protect its data and adhere to regulations. It makes sense: a company shouldn't really do any security exercises unless they know why or how they should do them.

Once defined, then security goes next. It takes the policies and procedures as an input to guide the implementation of protection. Security is the actual act. For those new to this world, this is a big insight to understand: unless you know the specific policies and procedures guiding security implementation, then you are simply doing security for the sake of security. It's not tied to anything, and it should be in order to properly fulfill regulatory responsibilities.

After implementation, that's where compliance comes in. Compliance is really the act of validating that security was implemented in the manner defined by a privacy role.

Understanding the maturity model is one of the best shortcuts to expertly understanding compliance's role in an organization.

Technical and administrative controls

HIPAA rules, typically interpreted as either privacy-based rules or security-based rules, are spread across the entire Omnibus. Splitting these rules in that way can be confusing since it doesn't accurately scope the technical concern for cloud technology. Therefore, when mapping controls to the rules, the best way for a cloud-based organization to interpret the rules is to split them into two groups: *technical* controls and *administrative* controls.

Technical controls[5] are all controls where a mechanical or digital process is required. Encryption is a basic example while datacenter maintenance is a much more nuanced implementation. For the purposes of isolating and describing cloud compliance, one can consider physical controls as a portion of technical controls. Experienced compliance officers will find that combination too narrow, and they are correct, but it is a helpful way to understand the complexity of cloud service abstraction explained throughout the book. A cloud organization can view most technical controls as requirements for its compliance management program, but not all. For example, software applications need not worry about compliance related to X-ray machines.

Administrative controls[6] are all controls that require a business process to implement, and usually matter to an organization. For example, HIPAA requires companies to train their employees annually, or to manage passwords a certain way. Some administrative controls, like the controls surrounding access, apply differently to cloud-based companies that must manage authentication and authorization as a business process through all layers of the cloud computing stack, including within the business itself.

How assurance works: audits and assessments

Since its enactment in 1996, HIPAA and its corresponding audits have been consistently completed in the same way. Unfortunately, that process is conducted differently by everyone who administers the audits.

Keep in mind third-party validation matters because a key driver for Covered Entities conducting business with Business Associates is assurance. Blend everything discussed so far, like controls and maturity models, and the result is assurance. Organizations managing risk care deeply about mitigating the risk, especially when working with partners. Consequently, in order to provide assurance, a business typically engages with an auditing firm who routinely takes its home-baked auditing framework, based on its personal

interpretations of HIPAA, and audits the business based on their parameters. At the end of the audit, the auditor returns the results and the process
concludes.

The problem is obvious. For more than twenty years, thousands of organizations have argued that their interpretation of HIPAA is the right interpretation. Few facts contribute more to the stale state of health IT than this one.
Finger pointing at the U.S. healthcare system is inadequate. A nonstandard
third-party legal interpretation that facilitates an audit of a non-prescriptive
regulation is an inefficiency plaguing every regulated industry worldwide.

Fortunately, some parties are injecting standardization into the interpretation
process, thus helping business engagements to become more transactional.
HITRUST is a U.S. healthcare industry-led attempt at creating a more
prescriptive and consistent framework[7].

Frameworks to the rescue

For companies on an innovation trajectory, compliance becomes crucial for
the regimes of their vertical or geography. Vendors can't proclaim compliance
based on a self-audit or self-assessment. Companies must somehow demonstrate compliance with third-party validation and verification. In financial
services, PCI-DSS comes into play. For public entities, internal controls and
security requirements are written into Sarbanes Oxley (SOX), a U.S. regulation, that must be reported to the SEC that requires management of certain
risk frameworks. In healthcare, HITRUST applies.

HITRUST Common Security Framework sets the bar

HITRUST was founded by a diverse set of organizations spanning different
sectors of healthcare who were looking for a prescriptive definition of HIPAA.
They banded together and initiated the HITRUST Alliance, an organization
that produces a normalized risk management framework, and a standard
process for assessing the risk posture of other organizations and technologies.
While a company can be HIPAA compliant, HIPAA certification does not exist;
that's the gap HITRUST addresses.

The strength of HITRUST is that it didn't create a framework from scratch.
To standardize a common, certifiable one that benefits both Covered Entities
and Business Associates, HITRUST created a meta framework out of multiple

existing legislation, regulation, and best practice frameworks, including the HIPAA Omnibus, ISO 27001, and NIST Special Publication (SP) 800-53[8].

This illustration, created by the authors of this book, is an abbreviated explanation of the evolution of compliance leading up to the birth of HITRUST to help tell the story of how different eras of technology have lead to new understandings of how to control that technology. While HITRUST is uniquely created on its own, it is interesting to observe how it has stood on the shoulders of giants like NIST, PCI, ISO 27000 series, GDPR, and COBIT, which in turn have drawn inspiration since the turn of the twentieth century. The result is a framework in prime position to help companies adapt to the dynamic nature of the cloud.

The lineage of HITRUST also demonstrates how major compliance events are tied to major technology spans. HIPAA was developed when PCs using Windows in a networked environment began dominating every desk in America, which meant the concept of private information being hacked off hard drives from afar became a reality. In an earlier decade, stolen PHI was confined to manual theft from a filing cabinet. In this new digital world, protecting patient privacy took center stage and government administrators designed the HIPAA Rules to help organizations achieve that goal. In that regard, observing that HITRUST CSF v1 was developed during the advent of the public cloud is a good indicator that its design fits modern times.

Using the HITRUST CSF

Similar in structure to ISO 27001:2005, HITRUST CSF v9.1 released in 2018 consists of 14 Control Categories, 49 Control Objectives and 149 total Control Specifications, which provide organizations with a giant catalog of controls that can be tailored to their needs based on specific organizational, system and regulatory risk factors. The HITRUST CSF has been updated at least annually since 2010 to incorporate changes in existing sources, such as the most recent ISO 27001 release in 2013, and incorporate new sources relevant to industry, such as GDPR, which also explains why the total number of available control requirements fluctuates with every release.

Instead of conducting an audit using a proprietary framework developed by an independent consultant, organizations can ask their auditor or assessor to use the HITRUST CSF.

Standing on the Shoulders of Giants

A few of the many influences that created
HITRUST's CSF

ISACA
1967

NBS
1901

N
19

AIPCA
1887

MIL
Q9850
1959

ISO/IEC
9000
1987

IEC
1906

ISO
1947

ISO/IEC
JTC 1
1987

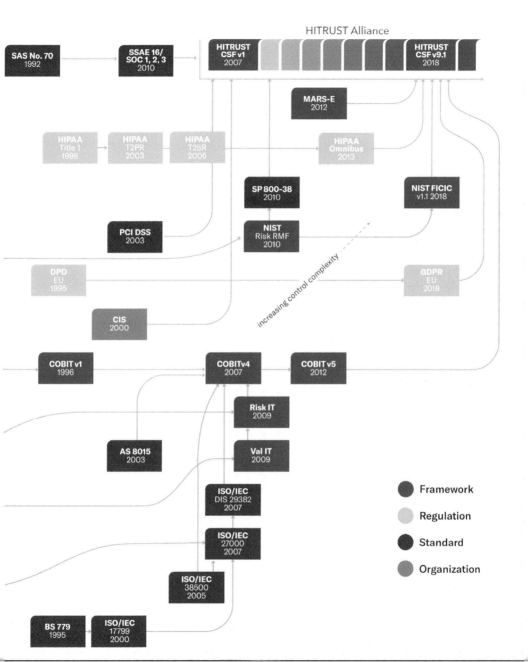

HITRUST Alliance

SAS No. 70 1992 → SSAE 16/ SOC 1, 2, 3 2010 → HITRUST CSF v1 2007 ... HITRUST CSF v9.1 2018

MARS-E 2012

HIPAA Title 1 1996 → HIPAA T2PR 2003 → HIPAA T2SR 2005 → HIPAA Omnibus 2013

SP 800-38 2010

NIST FICIC v1.1 2018

PCI DSS 2003

NIST Risk RMF 2010

DPD EU 1995

GDPR EU 2018

CIS 2000

increasing control complexity

COBIT v1 1996 → COBIT v4 2007 → COBIT v5 2012

Risk IT 2009

AS 8015 2003

Val IT 2009

ISO/IEC DIS 29382 2007

ISO/IEC 27000 2007

ISO/IEC 38500 2005

BS 779 1995 → ISO/IEC 17799 2000

● Framework
● Regulation
● Standard
● Organization

The CSF supports three means of assessment. Organizations can do a self-assessment, which is useful for an initial gauge on compliance posture. However, self-assessments aren't externally useful since they aren't conducted by an independent third party. This is the second form of assessment: i.e., a third-party assessor firm is used to help conduct the assessment, which may or may not be submitted to HITRUST for validation. If the assessor firm is an HITRUST approved assessor, then the organization's assessment can be submitted to the HITRUST Alliance itself, which can either validate or certify the assessment based on the results and associated scoring. Organizations should ultimately strive for a HITRUST Alliance Certified assessment.

Assessment scoping is a big part of the process. Organizations need not include all the control requirements in the catalog. The requirements are tailored to an organization based on specific organizational, system, and regulatory risk factors to help ensure only those that are relevant are included in the assessment—a digital health company, for example, has no concern for control requirements related to physical hardware installed in a hospital room. The assessment also only addresses a subset of controls in order to provide relying parties a reasonable level of assurance about the organization's security program at a reasonable cost to the organization.

CSF assessments are conducted every two years with an interim evaluation of the relevant scope to ensure corrective actions, if any, are making progress and there are no significant changes to the organization or its systems that might impact the assurances provided by the assessment. HITRUST is also working with industry representatives to define an industry-standard approach to shared responsibility and the inheritance of controls from a cloud provider's CSF assessment by their customers. This will allow relying parties to obtain the same benefits for cloud-based services they currently receive from more traditional business partners and vendors that leverage the HITRUST CSF.

Cloud-specific compliance: CSA STAR

Another organization and certification with specific relevance for the cloud is the Cloud Security Alliance (CSA) Security, Risk, and Assurance Registry (STAR)[9]. CSA STAR is based on the Cloud Controls Matrix (CCM), written and maintained by the CSA, with three levels of certification—self certified, verified, and continuous. Like with the HITRUST CSF, CCM is mapped to other frameworks, including HITRUST, Fedramp, PCI, AICPA SOC, and HIPAA.

The interesting aspect of the CSA CCM and the CSA STAR program is its cloud specificity means certain aspects of the cloud are built into the CSA framework. The CCM adopts the concept of Shared Responsibility and builds it into the framework. They do so to capture the reality that, on the cloud, some security controls are the responsibility of the cloud provider, some are the responsibility of the cloud customer, and some are shared. Additionally, deployment models like SaaS, PaaS, and IaaS are also captured; with the lines blurred between these deployment services, mapping controls to one model or another is increasingly difficult and even potentially irrelevant. CSA addresses that obscurity.

Financing the future

Despite common perceptions, compliance is a business problem; not a technology problem. Part of the business case of compliance relates to the business user—in this instance, a compliance officer—who influences technology strategy. Helping the compliance officer understand cloud technology or helping the technologist understand the business constraints of compliance are key to converting compliance into an organizational asset.

Finance offers a helpful analogy. Throughout the last several years, the cloud has shifted from a costly toy to a key driver of business outcomes. Along the way, financiers got involved with infrastructure decision making. "Run your cloud like a business" is a phrase proffered by Cloudability, a leading cloud financial and operational management platform. That phrase summarizes the key shift brought by the discipline of finance.

"Some companies are consciously moving money from CapEx into R&D so they can build more products," mentioned Mat Ellis, CEO and founder of Cloudability. "The people who are proposing this and showing results are the executives getting promoted because they're increasing the speed of innovation for no extra money. They're literally making R&D out of thin air."

The industry has a long way to go for a fuller and more confident implementation, however. Ellis explains, "Right now people are using the cloud, but they're not willing to do the work to control it, either through compliance or financial controls."

The lessons learned between compliance and finance are stark. Organizations must treat compliance like a business problem, and not a technical one, similar to what finance officers do through the help of tools like Cloudability, where cloud cost management is correspondingly treated as a business problem and less a technical one. Upon doing so, organizations save money to reinvest in innovation to deliver a better, faster, or more-capable product.

"The six percent of U.S. company costs that were spent on IT in the form of upfront CapEx and OpEx are now moved to cash. Those parts should be treated like the rest of the business," continues Ellis. "That means, measured constantly with the goal of driving continual spend improvement to enable the business to accomplish more with less. Only then can an improved product experience positively impact the business."

Just like finance, compliance is not a set-it-and-forget-it problem. Continuous management and optimization of compliance is required to do it correctly. Yet, compliance needs an entirely new approach to resource allocation in the context of the cloud, just like how Cloudability helped businesses continuously monitor cloud expenses in order to divert savings into new initiatives.

"Basically, we just have to go from working at NASA to working at SpaceX. Instead of doing a moonshot initiative to alter the product or service offerings once every decade, successful companies do it every week. You have to run your technology like you run your business. Understand the unit cost and try and drive it down, as well as make savvy decisions around whether you add a feature, lower the price or increase the profit margin," said Ellis.

The business case for compliance is similar. A company must run its compliance program like it runs its business, which means designing in dexterity to adjust to new trends. Upon doing so, the technology and administrative costs to maintain legacy software can be transformed into cash to reinvest into improving the business.

What makes compliance essential?

Compliance is a very broad concept that industry-by-industry and domain-by-domain might take different forms with different intents.

Think of compliance like the guardrails on a curvy road. When not present, the drive gets dangerous. Well, business transactions are twisted journeys.

In regulated industries, the only trust that exists is the natural trust of one party with another, and sometimes those parties become bad actors. That's where schemes, fraud, and over-leveraged deals arise. The reason why compliance exists, and why some industries are much more regulated than others, is because those industries are the ones where the most catastrophic damage to a society or individuals can happen if bad actors are in play. A swell of digital data about individuals is produced daily. Now, the lines are blurring. As a result, broad-brush regulations like GDPR now apply to all organizations that capture, process, or store individual information.

With compliance and the cloud, all roads lead back to privacy and security issues. It could be literal, in a technological sense, like encryption, but all policies for humans relate to the same thing—security. For example, best practices suggest using Access Control Lists (ACLs), a term that defines who can access certain systems on a server, and to what someone with a password sees when logging into an app, all the way up to how businesses manage and train employees. It all ties back to data security.

Compliance on the cloud, then, is the process of proving security *of*, *on*, and *in* the cloud. While we get into more depth about the specific meanings later, *of* can be thought of as the physical layer, *on* can be thought of as the host layer, and *in* can be thought of as everything within the host. It's how one organization gives assurances about best practices being used for security implementation to other organizations, be they partners, customers, or regulators. The compliance must-haves are essentially a proxy for privacy must-haves and security must-haves.

Compliance rules are drafted by lawyers and regulators, not necessarily technologists. While some technological definitions found within regulatory rules are inefficient or obsolete, the reasoning behind the rules are straightforward and correct. Implementing updated processes or controls to match the spirit of the rules, then getting those controls validated by a third party, is the right approach to compliance by a modern technology company. Trust is earned through validations of controls.

Therefore, compliance can be a litmus test for organizational integrity, which is why it's viewed as an irritant by organizations without resources, time, or the patience to go through the process of understanding what compliance means. For better or worse, a three-person Silicon Valley startup building a digital health app at a weekend hackathon will find compliance a burden, whereas Fortune 100 enterprises view compliance as a cornerstone to their global business operations.

Add to that the continuous, always-on nature of compliance on the cloud, and compliance becomes expensive because it's a process that acts essentially as a cycle. Compliance is set up and then a company must prove it is set up the right way. Then it's managed and updated on an ongoing basis. One of those rules in the HIPAA Omnibus, for example, is the act of scanning for intrusions. Are there pings coming in from computer consoles in China, Russia, North Korea? Are people attacking an organization? That's called intrusion detection, or IDS. Tracking that, reviewing the logs, and analyzing what kind of activity is coming in are rote daily tasks.

Compliance as an asset

Compliance may seem like an onerous and unnecessary chore to please micromanaging lawyers and regulators, but that view is one-sided. Compliance is not simply a checkbox to get past. Compliance is an enabler or an asset instead of a blocker or liability. An organization, developer, or even a compliance officer must transmute the limiting view of compliance to an expanded one.

When an organization solves the problem of compliance and clearly demonstrates it, the organization can embrace the cloud and enable digital transformation, thus becoming a trusted industry leader, partner, and innovator. With compliance as an enabler of the cloud, organizations can fundamentally shift the role of IT from a bottleneck or cost center into a strategic voice in the C-suite and boardroom.

The modern and future cloud is about leveraging partners. The next chapter will examine the way in which to use partnerships to an organizational advantage. The reliance on partners and models of Shared Responsibility, make compliance an even more powerful asset for any organization. To use that asset wisely, organizations must fundamentally shift their view of compliance.

Instituting a holistic program to manage compliance of, on, and in the cloud is the secret to turning the cloud into an engine for organizational innovation. Understanding what the cloud is today compared to the past and what it will be in the future is the first step.

CHAPTER 3

What *Really* is the Cloud?

And *where* is it, exactly?

Contrary to simple infographics of the past, depicting a fluffy cloud to describe data moving from one desktop computer terminal to another, information simply doesn't float above one's head ready to be plucked when needed. The cloud is traditionally explained as "somebody else's hard drive on the internet." But that's the old definition. The cloud's modern definition is much more complex. Essentially, the modern cloud is a hardware utility delivered to customers as software-based managed services – i.e., computer resources like compute power, storage (block, file, and blob), container orchestration, big data tools, all packaged as APIs or interactive products delivered to cloud customers as software, not hardware.

Large public cloud service providers (CSPs) no longer simply sell caged hardware from a remote data center. These providers have developed specific software that runs across large fleets of global hosts, offering scaling and geographic reach with simple commands. The cloud is no longer somebody else's computer; it's a different way to consume computer resources based on software, not hardware. The hardware of the cloud, built by the CSPs with billions of dollars of investment, is in place. We are now living in a post-cloud world. And our post-cloud world is increasingly based on managed services, not remote hardware, dedicated instances, hard drives, or VMs.

The modern cloud, delivered via managed services, fundamentally changes the approach to costs, scale, liability, and delivery. Organizations can now operate at global scale, delivering digital solutions and collecting digital data, without a physical presence in each geography. The cloud provides benefits like elasticity, shared resources, resiliency, and global availability that all contribute to the trifecta of lower IT costs, faster business processes, and increased availability. The cloud has become a transformative force that is reshaping whole industries, not just technology.

While the concept of treating computing resources, or primitives, like a utility has been around since the 1960s, by the 2000s, the IT industry began seeing more processing power, memory, and applications being hosted in remote data centers. Large technology companies like Microsoft, Amazon, IBM, and Google reached a point where they had sprawling global infrastructure with millions of servers and the capacity to lease computing resources to other businesses. By 2006, these companies began aggressively positioning the term "cloud computing" to indicate when people accessed software, compute power, and files remotely over the web instead of on their desktops.

91%
of organizations are concerned about cloud security.

Source: 2018 Cloud Security Report of 570 cybersecurity professionals.

Some industries adopted cloud computing quickly, like gaming and retail, which coincided with the mobile revolution sparked by the 2007 introduction of the Apple iPhone. Incidentally, those early adopter industries also had the fewest compliance headaches. Highly-regulated industries like finance and healthcare have been slower to migrate to the cloud, largely due to concerns over stringent security and privacy requirements. A 2018 report by Crowd Research Partners asked 570 cybersecurity professionals about their cloud views, and the results confirmed these anxieties: 91% said they had security concerns about data hosted on the cloud[10].

Despite those concerns, a recent boom has arisen in startup-driven digital technology within regulated industries, thanks to rising pressures of cost curtailment and enabling new partnerships while improving the quality of customer (or patient) experiences that transcend the conservative nature of these industries.

With the explosion of digital data, the advent of mobile-first societies, and the increased market demand of the cloud, businesses ranging from hospitals to banks to insurance companies and pharmaceuticals have been collecting petabytes of data about their customers. Systems of record have gone digital, yet remained siloed from each other in different departments and technologies and can be extremely difficult to integrate. Moreover, an explosion of new data generated both passively as well as actively with new sensor-based tools, commonly called the "Internet of Things" has erupted. A convergence of paradigm shifts has led every industry and company to rethink its business models from the ground up.

Some of the most important and sweeping trends require intense amounts of data, such as targeted advertising in social media, customer tracking in software tools, precision medicine and population health in healthcare, or credit scores and personalized investment plans in finance. The kind of infrastructure required for this data deluge pushes the envelope of older on-premises capabilities institutions have in place today.

This places intense pressure to explore the benefits of moving to the cloud and start developing a cloud roadmap for established enterprises in all industries.

The three verbs of compliance: store, compute, transmit

One can get lost in the intricacies of deployment or service models. A quick way to grasp the totality of the cloud is through understanding the actions committed upon data. Terminology varies from compliance regime to compliance regime, but, in general, all rules come back to these three verbs associated to data: store, compute, and transmit.

Store. This is the simplest verb. There are different characteristics for digital data storage—persistent, ephemeral, and, in memory, volatile and non-volatile. In all cases, compliance addresses the risk associated to the length of storage and ways storage can be accessed. Engineers might create their own data storage solution on top of a server using a popular database, but managed storage services are very popular cloud services today, such as Amazon S3 or Microsoft Azure SQL Database. There are countless HIPAA violations[11] resulting from improperly securing storage devices.

Compute. All computer use cases come back to compute processes using cores or other parts of the technology stack associated to CPU or, increasingly, GPU units. Meltdown and Spectre[12] are two recent, very high profile threats that targeted hardware processors and the process verb to gain unauthorized access to data.

Transmit. Simply, this is sending data from one place to another. With the cloud, there are now countless end points sending and receiving data. The most common form of protection is encryption, or specifically encryption in transit, from end to end. VPNs are a commonly used, if burdensome, form of secure connections in regulated industries. The most common form of attack in transit is a man in the middle (MITM) attack[13].

THE LANGUAGE OF DATA

In a data-driven future, it's important to think about what constitutes an API. One simple way to think about APIs is through the semantics of nouns and verbs, just like a sentence. At a very basic level, a typical API will list a collection of nouns, like `Patient` or `Appointment`, and available verbs someone can call to interact with the nouns, like `getPatient(ID)` or `setAppointment(timestamp)`. Documented and accessible nouns and verbs available in an API is the way interoperable data models are created.

There are certainly many more actions that engineers will enact on private or generic data than **store, compute,** and **transmit.** One example is **secure:** Engineers must do a lot of things to data to ensure it is secure, like encrypt it and back it up.

So why is the book simplifying to just three verbs, so to speak? A key insight this book attempts to communicate is that the highest order actions committed on regulated data are store, compute, and transmit: the data has to live somewhere, then be processed via some logic, then move between locations. To solve compliance, engineers should be thinking about how they address controls across those three foundations.

How the cloud works

Confusion has deepened about what cloud computing is, how to leverage it, who is using it, and why it is appealing relative to other models of computing.

A good way to understand the elements of cloud computing is to look at how the National Institute of Standards and Technology (NIST), part of the U.S. Department of Commerce, breaks it down. NIST has identified five essential characteristics, three service models, and four deployment models to explain the cloud[14].

1. Cloud Characteristics

The essential characteristics of cloud computing include:

On-demand self-service   Users of cloud computing are able to access the computing resources they need—such as processing time, storage, and bandwidth—by themselves.

Broad network access   Cloud computing resources can be utilized by remote clients using standard mechanisms. Think of web applications and the APIs needed to build them.

Resource pooling   Computer resources are dynamically shared across many clients and cloud-deployed apps, helping to keep costs down.

Rapid elasticity   This is extremely powerful as it enables apps to scale up cloud computing resources as needed, on-demand, to support peaks and troughs of usage, instead of having to build and support high-powered resources and service 24/7.

Measured service   Usage is metered, and cloud computing is typically billed on a per-use basis. In the case of pure infrastructure, little-to-no money is wasted because users only pay for what they consume, such as bandwidth, storage, or user accounts.

2. Service Models

The service models of cloud computing define the amount of control customers have over the infrastructure.

SERVICE MODELS AT A GLANCE

Infrastructure-as-a-Service (IaaS). Infrastructure-as-a-Service is central to cloud strategies. Now that so much data is collected by digital solutions, wearables, and sensors, IaaS is used to store, backup, and ultimately analyze that data in the cloud.

Platform-as-a-Service (PaaS). Platform-as-a-Service on the cloud is leveraged by developers to quickly deploy and scale their applications in a cloud-based environment.

Software-as-a-Service (SaaS). SaaS is a cloud service model for accessing hosted applications developed by a vendor.

Infrastructure-as-a-Service (IaaS). Infrastructure-as-a-Service is central to cloud strategies. Now that so much data is collected by digital solutions, wearables, and sensors, IaaS is used to store, backup, and ultimately analyze that data in the cloud. Analyst firms like Gartner are now calling this layer Cloud Service Providers or CSPs, even though CSP typically means companies providing services on the cloud, because IaaS vendors are increasingly creeping "up the stack" to provide more services on top of themselves. Consequently, CSPs at this layer are sometimes referred to as "hyper-scale CSPs" to delineate their difference from typical "X-as-a-Service" cloud service providers.

CSPs are usually the cheapest option when compared to on-premise computing, as evidenced by the remarkably cheap compute costs with vendors like AWS or Microsoft Azure. IaaS is a blank slate, and developers can customize down to the operating system level. CSPs are racing to launch more primitives, or specific IaaS services, in which customers piece together, build and deploy their technology. Initially, IaaS created primitives for basic compute and storage, but are now branching into more managed services for things like databases, containers, and even machine learning. Each has an eye on being the central utility for the inevitable future age of artificial intelligence.

As CSPs launch more and more managed services, lines become blurred between IaaS and PaaS, and to a lesser extent SaaS. CSPs are no longer synonymous with IaaS, as the unbundling of physical hardware into software delivered services is shifting more control to IaaS. And, here's the result: PaaS is now often used to mean different things, from traditional PaaS like Heroku to simple managed databases. The mixing of terms is creating more market confusion which needs to be managed for understanding and ensuring compliance on the cloud.

With increased control comes increased responsibility, and ultimately more time spent on configuring and maintaining infrastructure for IaaS customers. The decision facing most engineering teams typically centers on the convenience of PaaS or control of IaaS. IaaS is more work than PaaS for the customer but provides more flexibility, so the answer along that spectrum is usually contextual to how the business views technology ownership for technology reasons, like eliminating lock-in or accelerating development cycles. Compliance reasons can also arguably be a factor.

In the options for IaaS, the industry has consolidated around American CSPs like AWS, Microsoft Azure, Google Cloud Platform, IBM SoftLayer, and Oracle, with Alibaba making a strong international push. Market analysts project CSPs at the IaaS layer to creep higher into PaaS and SaaS territory with their product offerings.

Platform-as-a-Service (PaaS). Platform-as-a-Service on the cloud is leveraged by developers to quickly deploy and scale their applications in a cloud-based environment.

As a PaaS customer, you may have some control over the infrastructure, but it is limited. Users of PaaS typically do not have access to the underlying operating system or network devices. Developer customers of PaaS can focus on the application, written in a language of their choice, without worrying about building and maintaining the server to run it. The original value proposition for PaaS promised the elimination of humans to do developer operations (DevOps).

The most common example is Heroku, a PaaS founded in 2007 that is now a part of Salesforce. Others include CloudFoundry or dozens of newer offerings like dotCloud. In healthcare, a few PaaS options exist to explicitly manage HIPAA compliance risks at this layer of the technology stack.

Software-as-a-Service (SaaS). Many consumer-facing digital solutions are offered as Software-as-a-Service. In finance, SaaS products might be finance trackers or credit monitoring apps. For enterprise businesses, think customer relationship management tools (CRMs), marketing automation, secure messaging, and helpdesk software. In healthcare, SaaS might be a portal allowing access to personal health records, a mobile app to monitor heart rates, or a backend solution for hospitals such as HR software. SaaS is the most limited model of cloud computing in terms of customer control. The SaaS vendors manage the entirety of the technology stack for their products.

SaaS is a cloud service model for accessing hosted applications developed by a vendor. Typical access is gained through a web app, mobile app, or an API, and is usually billed by user, API calls, or seats. Billing is subscription-based, or recurring.

Subscription-based models have implications for customers because of the low capital expense to get started, and implications for SaaS vendors because of the high negative upfront cash flow outlay to grow. The classic example of a SaaS is Salesforce, which allows businesses to manage customer relationships. The amount of other SaaS vendors today is overwhelming, with more started every day. Pick a product brand—Dropbox, Zendesk, MailChimp, Office 365, Gmail, the list goes on forever—and it's SaaS.

3. Deployment Models

Next, look at the various cloud deployment models, which define the expanse of the group sharing the cloud computing resources.

Private cloud. Private cloud infrastructure is dedicated hardware used exclusively by one entity and can be located on or off the premises of the entity. Based on trends in the 2010s, most larger enterprises will move from aging self-owned data centers to vendor-specific private clouds, including highly regulated and risk-averse industries like healthcare and finance. The challenge with most current private cloud deployments is in the area of capabilities. A public cloud provides auto-scaling, API-based access to perform maintenance and management, and so on. Private clouds don't typically offer these options.

Community cloud. In this deployment, infrastructure is shared with a group, or community of users and organizations. This can be viewed as a shared private cloud and is usually a community that has something in common.

Public cloud. This is the infrastructure that developers know best. In this deployment model, the physical infrastructure, and the software services, or primitives offered on top of it, is for public use, and resides solely on the premises of the cloud service provider.

Hybrid cloud. This model is comprised of a mix of two different deployment models from above. With a hybrid cloud approach, an organization owns some of the infrastructure while accommodating spikes in needed computing resources by offloading specific workloads to the public cloud. Hybrid models are usually viewed as the bridge for enterprises to migrate fully to the public cloud.

The most common solution to hybrid computing today consists of VPNs, or secure tunnels to connect cloud-based and ground-based environments. VPNs can and do require constant care, something that needs evaluation while assessing the total cost of ownership for cloud environments. In addition, new approaches to hybrid cloud computing are emerging and those will be discussed later in this chapter.

When referencing "the cloud" in this book, the authors mean the public cloud unless stated otherwise. The public cloud is where the majority of cloud-native services are offered, both today and into the future, which is why new businesses immediately start on the public cloud. For the next several years, most enterprise organizations will consume the cloud in hybrid models with private cloud and public cloud workloads humming side-by-side. Over time, trends indicate hybrid enterprises will gradually shift a greater proportion of workloads to the public cloud due to the superior experience and lower costs available to microservice-based architectures.

The post-cloud world is for software developers, not operators

The first versions of the cloud used to be hardware in somebody else's data center. This hardware was remotely managed, could scale up or down on demand, and had major benefits based on managing the physical technology infrastructure (power, internet, HVAC, physical security, processors, hard drives and tape drives, etc). This hardware version of the cloud empowered operators like "sys admins", database administrators, and others with similar roles. The smallest atomic unit was typically a virtual machine (VM). It also enabled shifting IT budgets from capital expenditures to operating expenses. This was not a distant past; it was 5–10 years ago.

Fast forward to today, 2018, and the cloud is not about hardware in somebody else's data center, it's about software enabled infrastructure services. Yes, those software-based infrastructure services, or cloud services or cloud managed services, are run on hardware in somebody else's data center. But those managed services are delivered in software layers abstracted from the underlying hardware. The smallest atomic unit is not a VM a managed service running across a fleet of hosts; examples are things like database as a service (DBaaS), container orchestration services, API-services, etc. In this abstracted model delivered as software, the current and future version of the cloud empowers software developers and not operators.

Organizations leveraging today's software-delivered cloud offload not just physical technology infrastructure, but operations for that hardware. It's the reason why the leading CSPs are hiring armies of operators.

This software, or cloud services model, breaks down barriers to deploying and scaling new technology. At the same time, it opens up a world of new vulnerabilities as developers not only build new technology but also, via cloud services, configure the security of their own environments.

In 2018, the hardware cloud utility is in place. This hardware is foundational but is not the true transformative power of the cloud. The true power of the cloud is managed services built to empower software developers. It is safe to say we are now living in a post-cloud world. Now is the race to create more software services, or managed services, for developers to enable specific technology use cases.

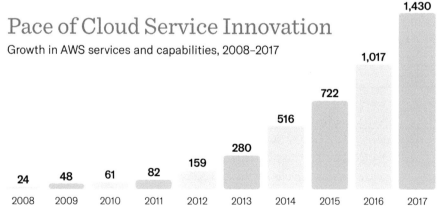

Pace of Cloud Service Innovation

Growth in AWS services and capabilities, 2008–2017

2008	2009	2010	2011	2012	2013	2014	2015	2016	2017
24	48	61	82	159	280	516	722	1,017	1,430

Data from AWS presentation, *2017 re:Invent Conference*

CSPs are racing to launch more software primitives in which customers combine, build and deploy their technology. This image, with data taken from an AWS session at the 2018 AWS re:Invent conference, demonstrates the rapid pace of available services on their cloud. Azure and GCP service growth has had similar trajectories. It's insanely fast.

Where is that service growth happening? Today software delivered services are branching into categories like databases, containers, container orchestration, and even machine learning. Each CSP has an eye on being the central utility for the inevitable future age of artificial intelligence.

As CSPs launch more managed services, lines become blurred between IaaS and PaaS, and to a lesser extent SaaS. CSPs are no longer synonymous with IaaS, as the unbundling of physical hardware into software delivered services is shifting more control to IaaS. And, here's the result: PaaS is now often used to mean different things, from traditional PaaS like Heroku to simple managed databases. The mixing of terms is creating more market confusion which needs to be managed for understanding and ensuring compliance on the cloud.

Despite the confusion and growing pains in the post-cloud world, managed services are here to stay. The great cloud hardware to software unbundling will continue at breakneck speed for the foreseeable future, powering armies of software developers to invent the future.

This rapid shift to managed services has huge implications for security and compliance, most notably the diminishing role of system administrators and database administrators, and to a lesser extend DevOps, within a typical AWS, Azure, or GCP customer. In fact, the opposite is true: those role are more important to the CSPs themselves. With managed services, software developers are able to deploy and scale their own infrastructure, meaning those software developers are now responsible for securing managed services to comply with compliance regimes. The typical checks of security and compliance for new infrastructure are often being circumvented through the use of managed services. This is a hard problem that is made more difficult to solve as managed services, and the configuration of those services, are changing all the time.

Moving regulated information to the cloud

Regulated entities are working to make the transition to the cloud with as few disruptions as possible. Migration happens less frequently than everyone would hope because it is filled with complexities and difficult tradeoffs. When migration does occur, it happens the same way in slow-paced industries as it happened in the 2000s: through data connections between legacy systems and new cloud-based solutions.

The onramp for healthcare to the cloud, for example, is about data control, not about simply lifting and shifting legacy systems out of hospital data centers and onto the cloud. Bottlenecks occur during the onramp, most notably data integration of electronic health records systems that have dominated health IT systems for the last 15 years.

Across all verticals, a resistance to migrating old systems to the cloud permeates. CIOs aren't interested in the downside, like higher hidden costs than the cloud vendor space indicates, high probability of downtime, failure of fragile systems during migration, and general unease with understanding compliance risks and liabilities on the cloud. As of 2018, hybrid deployment models offer strategic teams the best way to start migrating to the public cloud.

A threshold abides where it's more cost effective to move workloads to the cloud. As such, one goal of chief information officers (CIOs) is to calculate that threshold specific to their company. Once the economics make sense, IT teams will evaluate the details. In doing so, two sets of equations must be addressed and resolved: the cost of "net-new" things, and the cost to migrate IT and legacy data to the cloud.

For cost, security, and usability purposes, the public cloud is emerging as the most common and better choice.

The best performing companies clearly have a stronger, more holistic vision of how to migrate to the cloud than companies who cherry-pick certain workloads. The good news is this is where a hybrid approach can have a major positive impact: mixing and matching public cloud migration with private cloud legacies isn't a bad strategy. That's assuming a strong vision is foundational to the approach. Hybrid models can help be the on-ramp so teams don't feel like an all-or-nothing strategy is the only option available.

The new hybrid cloud

While the public cloud is the inevitable endgame, hybrid cloud models are a viable path today and in the near future. In fact, most large enterprises, especially risk-averse ones, deploy hybrid models more frequently than utilizing the public cloud.

Today, a hybrid cloud leverages multiple deployment models, which commonly include a combination of public cloud and either private cloud or on-premises infrastructure. As of 2018, hybrid has become the primary standard for enterprise organizations, leading to new solutions and approaches that help manage technology and workloads across multiple, hybrid environments.

Organizations are embracing a hybrid approach today and will likely maintain some degree of a hybrid path for the foreseeable future, and maybe forever. Here are the reasons why:

Scale of migration. The first reason for hybrid is simply the scale of technology and data, especially legacy technology that would need migration to the cloud. Most large organizations house hundreds or thousands of applications in their data centers. Many of those applications are legacy and do not port easily to a public cloud environment, or the value of the cloud is not realized if legacy applications are not re-architected. Large-scale migration to the cloud requires both time and resources that also require a multi-year timeline even at the most progressive and aggressive organizations.

Security and compliance. For particular types of data in certain industries, the public cloud is not an option because of the perceived threat to security and compliance. The cloud requires reliance on partners, which requires clear obligations at every level of the technology stack. Today, data processing and privacy agreements lag the technology. In time, this problem will be solved but it will not follow Moore's Law like technology progression.

Edge computing. Edge computing is the processing of data at or close to the source of data[15]. It is most relevant in cases where data is being produced and near-real-time decisions are made based on the data. Latency exists when sending and receiving data and that latency has a high cost in some environments. One example is a hospital and its intensive care unit (ICU). Monitors are continuously collecting patient data. That data is triggering alerts and care pathways. Basic processing of that continuous patient data should be done at the hospital or ICU as it is being collected. The data can, in parallel, be sent to the cloud for more intensive processing and archiving.

- AWS has created data transfer services, the most common being AWS

Storage Gateway and AWS Snowball, for both bulk and real time data. These services help organizations maintain consistency of data across hybrid environments[16].

- Google recently released Google Kubernetes Engine on-premises (GKE OnPrem), a platform that can be run in any data center and enables organizations to create and manage cloud-native, container-based environments across hybrid environments. Management of these environments is centralized on Google, regardless of the data center where the environments reside. Additionally, GKE OnPrem makes it easy to re-architect and test applications for the cloud before actually migrating them to the cloud[17].

- Microsoft offers Azure Stack, which enables organizations to use Azure cloud services in their own data center. Organizations can leverage this extensive set of services to create consistency between their on-premises technology and cloud workloads[18].

As hybrid is the new normal for organizational IT, more services will be introduced for easier consistency in maintenance, both in terms of operational and developer experience, as well as security and compliance.

Bridging all layers of the stack

As hardware is broken up and offered as specific software primitives, or managed services by CSPs, cloud customers move further away from the underlying hardware layer. Increasingly, the cloud is consumed as a software utility, not a hardware utility. Led by CSPs blending the lines between IaaS, PaaS, and SaaS, customers are now being abstracted away from the underlying layers of the technology stack. More abstraction means greater customer convenience but less control.

To grapple with the increase of abstracted services, CSPs provide the concept of *Shared Responsibility,* an idea Microsoft and AWS, in particular, have pioneered since the 2000s. Shared Responsibility essentially outlines which compliance liabilities associated to which abstractions are taken on by the CSP versus the customer of the CSP[19]. AWS elegantly delineates their responsibility as Security *of* the Cloud while AWS customers are responsible for Security *in* the Cloud. Microsoft lists obligations across seven definable

Shared Responsibility

COMPLIANCE
IN
THE
CLOUD

Administrative

External Audit
3rd Party Assessment
Business Continuity
Risk Analysis
Employee Training
Organizational Policies

Application

User-Generated Data
Access Management
Identity

COMPLIANCE
ON
THE
CLOUD

Protocols & Process

Password Management
Risk Management
Disaster Recovery
Data Backup

Tools

User Management
Intrusion Detection
Monitoring & Logging
Authentication

Testing

Penetration Testing
Vulnerability Scanning
Integrity

Operating Systems

At-Rest Encryption
Patching
Configuration

Networking

Subnetwork Segmentation
Routing
VPN
In-Flight Encryption

COMPLIANCE
OF
THE
CLOUD

Cloud Primitives

Network
Database
Storage
Compute

Physical Infrastructure

Firewall Hardware
Connectivity
Regionality
Hardware
Power Management
Data Center Security

and easy to understand tiers. All told, CSPs take on full responsibility of the physical layer, like data centers, while prompting customers to meet compliance requirements at the operating system level and higher where controls are owned by the CPS. It can be inconsistent.

Shared Responsibility leads to inheritance

With Shared Responsibility, a concept emerges in cloud compliance today called *control inheritance*[20]. The concept, pioneered by HITRUST, is now generally accepted as a model for approaching the different layers of the cloud technology stack and the responsibility of controls therein[21]. While still early and not yet universally adopted, control inheritance helps organizations to ensure full-stack compliance. Control inheritance explicitly addresses the need to inherit certain security and compliance controls in layers managed by third parties, in this case CSPs and cloud services providers.

The easiest control inheritance example is physical security. In every compliance regime multiple requirement exist on the physical security for technology assets. CSP data centers have physical security controls, such as badge ID or biometric authentication, to prevent unauthorized access to physical technology assets. When CSP customers leverage those data centers for IT resources, those customers inherit the physical security controls of the CSPs.

While physical security is the easiest example, the abstracted nature of the cloud today makes inheritance of some compliance controls a bit murky. Additionally, some compliance requirements, such as access controls, are multi-layer across the technology stack, meaning some of the responsibility for access controls falls to the cloud providers and some fall to the cloud customers. To account for this, different types of inheritance can now be found.

Complete Inheritance. In this case, the entire control is inherited by the cloud customer. Physical security is a good example.

Partial Inheritance. With this type of inheritance, the control at some layer of the technology stack is managed by the cloud provider and at other layers the control is managed by the cloud customer. Access controls and password management are a good example because those controls are spread across the entire cloud environment.

No Inheritance. The cloud customer is fully responsible for the compliance control. Workforce training is an example of this.

While HITRUST has control inheritance baked into the CSF, it is not explicitly defined in most cases. The most common scenario for inheritance is when a CSP, or consultant or other cloud service provider, completes a security questionnaire for an audit or a customer and takes responsibility for a specific control. This is not a very powerful use of inheritance and the subtlety of the informal nature is lost on most organizations. The future of compliance inheritance should be more explicit. Organizations should attest to ownership of compliance controls, either partially or completely, with an explicit tie to privacy agreements and liability.

Sharing the (work)load

Without question, employing the Shared Responsibility model is the best way to identify compliance responsibilities with cloud workloads.

The key challenge for cloud users is the space between the physical layer at the bottom and the end user of applications at the top. Effectively, the entirety of the operating system layer, along with all managed and microservices on top of it, is the responsibility of the CSP customer. This stark realization should prompt the new reality of compliance on the cloud: the cloud is increasingly becoming software-based, but CSPs inherently do not own risk at the operating system level and higher.

CHAPTER 4

Why Data Interoperability Matters

The *transmit* verb applied to data requires more attention because transferring data between environments, regardless of cloud service model, creates additional risk for organizations exchanging data. The more integration that occurs, the more liabilities organizations must manage.

But an axiom as true as any other is that the future requires interoperability between many services and data sets, whether those services are on the cloud or in private data centers. Cloud native architectures rule the day, which requires the integration of "microservices" offerings. Unfortunately, existing technology used by regulated companies is already woefully outdated and hard to update, mandating organizations consider new service providers.

As a common example, evolving market conditions have forced hospitals to offer remote patient care. The legacy EHR vendors have been slow to offer telehealth solutions, much slower than the speed hospitals need to move to meet market demand. Consequently, the majority of hospitals today that want to support telehealth buy a modern telehealth solution, like American Well or Teledoc, and fold it into their application mix, including integrating it with their legacy EHR. Each new adopted innovation, like telehealth, is subsequently a new point of data transmission and risk.

The first crucial question organizations must ask themselves is if they should adopt new innovations or avoid doing so to minimize risk. The second crucial question is, if they have decided to adopt new innovations, how do they ensure they are not creating new data silos. This is a true quandary that gets more complex the deeper one digs.

A (very short) history of EHRs explains the status quo

EHRs are the systems of record for the United States healthcare system and, increasingly, the entire world. In the United States, close to 100% of physician practices use EHRs[22]. The adoption of EHRs has spiked significantly over in the last 10 years due to federal incentives provided for Meaningful Use that were a part of the HITECH Act[23].

Federal administrators and industry leaders envisioned EHRs as a way to assist patient care by making data more readily available, facilitating better transitions in care, reducing redundant testing, and ultimately leading to better outcomes and lower costs. That was the theory, at least. There is limited data, and much dispute, on how to capture costs and savings of EHRs in practice[24]. The ROI and value of EHRs is debatable but the use of EHRs in modern medical practice is now guaranteed.

EHRs got their start in academia over 40 years ago. They were designed in an "episodic" care era of healthcare when patient care was provided in person, in episodes, often in large medical facilities or outpatient medical practices, in close proximity to large medical facilities; this is the era people often refer to as "episodic" care. This is still how most care in 2018 is delivered and, more importantly, how it is paid for in America. Payment amounts are based on the type of episode. More episodes, and the more higher paying codes attributed to each episode, result in more revenue funneled to care delivery organizations.

This is the health system that most major EHRs, including Epic and Cerner, were built to serve. Considering the alignment and tight coupling of EHRs with episodic care billing, it's no wonder that replacing EHRs would be high risk to top-line revenue during to the slow overall switch to value-based care.

The HITECH Act prompted consolidation of the best EHRs at the time, with the major winners being Epic, Cerner, and, to a lesser extent, Allscripts and Athena. Through this era with forced timelines of Meaningful Use, hospitals needed to be able to buy one product, or one platform. This consolidation resulted in the winning EHRs adding many new features to already large product suites. These features, which are mainly geared toward episodic care and operations of large medical systems, have created major bloat within today's EHRs.

This feature bloat can be best exemplified in the usage and interaction of clinicians with EHRs. One study found that physicians click within the EHR approximately 4,000 times during a 10-hour emergency room shift[25]. Much of that clicking is navigating to and from information buried deep in the bowels of massively bloated software built to do everything at a hospital. Other studies have found that physicians in the U.S. spend considerably more time in the EHR than caring for patients[26].

Another indirect result of HITECH was increased IT budgets at care delivery organizations[27], both the total spend and the IT spend as a proportion of overall organizational budget. In some cases, up to 80% of IT spend at care delivery organizations goes to installing, supporting, or optimizing EHRs.

EHRs aren't all bad. Prior to Meaningful Use, less than 10% of all patient records were digitized, meaning a year after the launch of the iPhone, 90% of patient records lived on paper stored in filing cabinets. EHRs did help to digitize records, which is a good thing.

Despite the recent explosion in EHR use the applications and technology that serve as the foundation for top EHRs are over 30 years old, sometimes older. Because of the underlying legacy nature of EHR technology, moving EHRs to the cloud presents significant challenges. This challenge of re-architecting EHRs for the cloud has beaten the inevitable path of healthcare to the hybrid cloud.

This background sets the stage for where we are today. HITECH prompted adoption of legacy software platforms for episodic care that are now the hubs of nearly all clinical workflows and clinical data but are near-impossible to integrate. Clinicians spend the majority of their time with EHRs, and EHRs consume an outsized portion of the overall organizational budgets for hospitals, specifically the IT budgets.

Healthcare is changing rapidly

However, transformation *is* happening, and it is being driven by the demands of patients and clinicians in the form of digital health. As the healthcare industry finds itself constrained by legacy software built for pay-for-service models, it looks to shifting certain clinical workflows outside the EHR in order to appease newer value-based care models. An explosion of digital health products outside the EHR has subsequently filled the void.

Market data has proven the case over the last several years. According to a research study from firm Rockhealth[28], 2018 venture investment in digital health is set to approach $7 billion, compared to $1.2 billion in 2011. Almost every conceivable corner of the care continuum has had entrepreneurs and intrapreneurs attempt to bring innovation and change: telehealth, care coordination, secure messaging, genetics, diagnostics, scheduling, supply chain, bundled payments, durable medical equipment, physical therapy, clinician note dictation, benefit management, clinical trials, medical adherence, and dozens more categories[29].

The monolithic EHRs of today are being unbundled by focused companies that have built modern digital health applications founded on the cloud; we are moving from one company, the EHR, delivering everything in an episodic, fee-for-service world to a pay-for-quality world with best-of-breed digital health products. Those digital health applications are built to transform an isolated problem and optimize the patient and provider experience to the standards all patients and clinicians expected in today's digital world. This unbundling of the EHR is a painful process as EHRs battle to maintain their stronghold on the enterprise but are not well suited to be data platforms for modern applications.

More than ever, data matters, and those new digital health products are too often locked out of adoption due to poor data interoperability with EHRs.

In order for regulated organizations like health systems to take advantage of the cloud, they must adopt new digital products whose data is being *stored*, *computed*, and *transmitted* outside the on-premises legacy software, like the EHR. Existing market conditions combined with legacy technology debt is forcing a strategy dilemma and compliance crisis that must be solved: adopt new products and manage more risk, or maintain the status quo and fall further behind?

The future is *data-driven* healthcare

Healthcare data today predominantly resides in EHRs and is considered clinical data. That data is used for direct clinical decision making, oftentimes manually by providers, and for billing for episodic care. This model of data use and storage is not compatible with a future based on quality, continuous care, precision medicine, and new partnerships.

The future of healthcare requires informed decisions not just on clinical care and billing, but on risk and prevention.

And a data-driven healthcare future will drive care via multiple data-rich sources:

- Clinical via EHRs
- Internet of Things devices (IoT)
- Genomics
- And images, like x-rays, etc.

Combining this data, and indexing the data on individuals, is the key to a healthcare specific kind of machine learning. (In healthcare "machine learning" is a generic and broad term for precision medicine.) It is the key to answering new questions, developing new drugs, and enabling new partnerships across the spectrum of healthcare.

Data-driven healthcare is long ways from where we are today, considering that data predominantly resides in silos. In the best case, usage is based on historical data and targeted at populations, not individuals. Little is based on real-time data. The chasm between today's episodic, non-integrated healthcare and data-driven healthcare needs a bridge; there will not be a magical day when the situation changes in an instant. That bridge is why interoperability matters today.

Connecting the cloud to the ground

Unfortunately, adopting new products is borderline impossible due to the persistence of pre-cloud era interoperability. In a pre-cloud world, data integration in healthcare was primarily required to connect legacy applications within on-premise data centers for care delivered in person, based primarily on discrete episodes. The major use cases included billing, clinical, lab, pharmacy, and scheduling. This legacy integration environment still exists today, but the shift to the cloud drives an entirely new set of data integration requirements for remote and virtual care, mobile and connected health, as well as continuous care.

Healthcare's digital transformation has started with applications that fall broadly into categories like care management, telemedicine, and clinical communications because they are the categories that have the most immediate impact on top-line revenue growth, operational cost cutting, and improved patient care. In order for these digital experiences to be leveraged by both providers and patients, the technologies must be integrated with the EHR.

To make things harder, a variety of EHRs exist, all with different versions, including additional on-premises variants customized to a hospital's specific needs. The famous historical anecdote that best illustrates this is found in a large West Coast health system that once had five different versions of Epic running throughout the system due to mergers, meaning a new digital health product would likely have to integrate with the same customer five different times. Even today, scaling a cloud-based digital health application, assuming integration with the EHR is required, mandates setting up and maintaining literally hundreds of customized legacy EHR connections and reinventing the wheel for each health system customer.

This is even more painful than it sounds. The current state of the art for EHR integration involves leveraging a legacy data standard called HL7 (Health Level-7) v2 based off a thirty-year-old protocol. Unfortunately HL7 is a "standard" that has been, in many instances, customized and the resulting data transmitted through a secure tunnel, typically a VPN. The process requires an experienced and capable technical and project management team to spend hundreds of hours over many months to coordinate and "go live". Integration is not REST and it's not HTTPS. No SDKs or APIs exist. Experienced developers outside of healthcare are often shocked and appalled to learn how this works.

When integrating new data generated by digital health applications back into the EHR, the limitations of EHRs become more striking. Writing back the data often means attaching static files, usually PDFs, to the medical record. These files get intermingled with thousands of notes in the patient chart, severely limiting the data's value and oftentimes only addressing medical legal requirements, not care decisions.

Yet, hope remains on the horizon. For the first time in twenty years, much of the industry is committed to a new data standard Fast Healthcare Interoperability Resources, or FHIR for short. FHIR will help, but it will not entirely solve the problem.

The exponential growth of digital data

Part of the digital transformation promise is based on the data which can be used to help organizations gain customer (or patient) and operational insights. But data is not valuable if it remains siloed.

The same cloud-based, customer and digital engagement applications that cause headaches for compliance will drive new digital business models based on the data they generate, both actively and passively. Similar to the revolutionization of digital advertising spurred on by tracking activities like customer usage and browsing data, healthcare will someday leverage digital health experience data to customize and better care at an individual level. Unfortunately, no standard platform for digital transformation exists, and none is on the forefront, which means current cloud data is created, stored, and isolated by individual applications littered across servers and CSPs.

To be sure, the largest software companies in the world are vying to become digital data hubs, with an eye on eventually layering in machine learning (ML) capabilities. In healthcare, EHRs are the current hubs of clinical data and workflows, specifically, and are pushing to be the data hubs of the future healthcare enterprises outside the clinical world. But none are successfully nearing the holy grail of a single data platform, although some inch closer every year.

Absent a single platform to rule them all, the challenge of data consolidation is tightly coupled with cloud adoption because modern cloud adoption unfailingly means combining many disparate cloud services at once. As a result, the big winners on the cloud will invariably offer tools to make combining and leveraging data easier for organizations. The layer of data integration on the cloud is potentially the hardest to secure while simultaneously being the biggest driver of digital transformation—a conundrum that the best companies understand how to manage.

Managing the conundrum begins first by planning for it. Paddy Padmanabhan, author of *Big Unlock: Harnessing Data and Growing Digital Health Businesses in a Value-based Care Era*, spoke about data-driven healthcare's digital transformation in the cloud and said: "When I look at digital transformation, I'm really looking at the white space being the landscape of last mile applications, the applications that are going to really enhance the patient experience or enable caregivers better."

In sharing his thoughts on transformation in regulated industries, Padmanabhan stressed that while designers and innovators are correct to focus on the end user, what gets lost too often is an understanding of how backend systems connect—especially on the cloud.

"For the organizational context, there's a lot of opportunity with back end functions such as finance, HR, and legal to digitize many of the processes, improve efficiencies and do them in a very user friendly, seamless way. But, by and large, when we talk about digital transformation in healthcare, people tend to look at impacting the patient and the caregiver, as opposed to backend processes. Innovators look at the patient first, caregiver next, which is fine, but I would argue they're both equally important, and just as important as the backend systems that connect the experiences," added Padmanabhan.

"In the context of health systems, the three main aspects to digital transformation are (1) engaging with patients and improving the engagements with patients; (2) increasing caregiver efficiency and increasing and improving the caregiver experience, as well; and (3) increasing operational efficiencies within the enterprise. So there's three diamond steps to digital transformation. Engaging patients, improving caregiver efficiencies and increasing organizational efficiencies," continued Padmanabhan, who then emphasized, "But all need to be connected, however."

Healthcare is an interesting case study of the global intersection of digital transformation and compliance due to the growth of data collection. As digital health products become more commonplace, the volume of new data and new threats will escalate. Society is creating more data in 2018 than in all the years that have preceded. Data is collected for everything—underwear can now measure sweat levels. Considering that protected data is growing exponentially by the exabyte (one billion gigabytes) month-over-month means there are more systems to think about, more systems to integrate, more systems to demonstrate compliance, more attack vectors for bad actors, and more risk to manage. Businesses can't keep up.

Multi-Dimensional Compliance on the Cloud

Cloud architectures are becoming more of a constellation of services with varied amounts of abstraction built in to benefit the experience of the user, which is a good thing for innovation. The challenge is the wide array of services means a motley collection of compliance postures that are hard to manage. The way to think about the problem is through multiple dimensions: breadth, depth, and volume of policies.

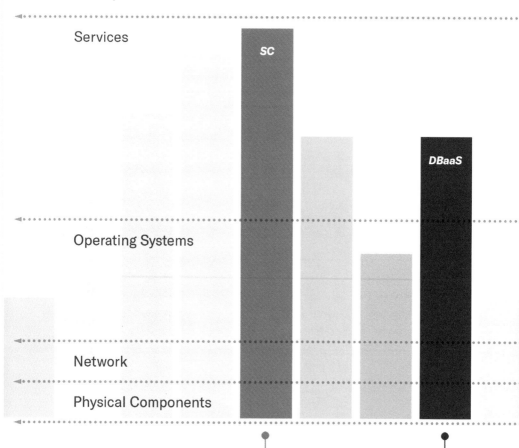

Services

SC

DBaaS

Operating Systems

Network

Physical Components

Serverless Computing

Users simply send a function call to a service to get a result. No need to manage anything server related.

Options include: AWS Lambda, Azure Functions, Google Cloud Functions

Database as a Service

Users have access to a database via APIs, but don't have to worry about managing versions, volumes, or other headaches.

Options include: Azure SQL Database, AWS RDS, Google Cloud SQL.

*Administrative
Policies & Procedures*
govern the full stack

Abstraction Tradeoff:
More Abstraction = Less Control
Less Abstraction = More Control

The more a service abstracts control
away from the user, the greater the
amount of controls the service must
manage on behalf of the user in
order to meet compliance.

e.g. HITRUST CSF
control *03.b Performing
Risk Assessments* which
maps to *HIPAA §
164.308(a)(1)(ii)(A)*

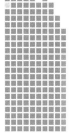

VM

MF

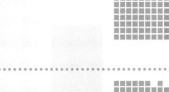

Managed Firewalls

Network traffic segmented by
firewalls is a notoriously hard
problem. Managed firewalls are a
tried and true solution.

*Options include: products from
Cisco, Barracuda, and Juniper
Networks.*

Virtual Machine Hosts

Virtual hosts sharing similar
physical resources but isolated for
multi-tenancy—a major inflection
point for cloud economics.

*Options include: VMware, Google
Cloud Managed VMs, AWS EC2,
and Azure VMs.*

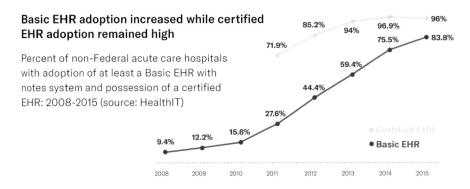

Basic EHR adoption increased while certified EHR adoption remained high

Percent of non-Federal acute care hospitals with adoption of at least a Basic EHR with notes system and possession of a certified EHR: 2008-2015 (source: HealthIT)

Placing investment bets is key for organizations like hospitals. Continued investment in old infrastructure at the expense of integrating new services is the exact calculus for disruptive innovation.

Some say the healthcare field may have already fallen too far behind. "Because all the big tech firms have done far more to make their infrastructure robust and compliant and ready than health systems ever will, health systems will never be able to catch up," Padmanabhan added. "The cloud is no longer an optional strategy, which enterprises are beginning to understand. Almost all legacy applications today are still on-premises, but many new investments are necessarily starting on the cloud first, so that's a good sign. The equation will more aggressively shift, maybe five years from now, when more applications are running on the cloud than not. It's starting mostly with discrete business functions such as enterprise analytics. But, overall, we're not there yet."

Adoption of the cloud allows health systems to integrate all the services and data used on the cloud, which is where the real value kicks in due to the promise of big data.

The future of artificial intelligence is here

Machine learning is on the upslope of the hype cycle for technology[30]. Correspondingly, machine learning, AI, and data analytics, are getting much attention and funding. And, rightfully so. Similar to the cloud, data analytics and machine learning will drive revolutionary changes in every industry.

The promise of machine learning in healthcare is greater than almost every other industry because the amount of relevant data points is likely greater than any other industry.

The health of individuals, and ultimately the objective effectiveness of healthcare, is primarily determined by a few things: genetics (aka nature), and the hundreds of individual interactions with our environment made everyday (aka nurture). It is really that simple. An additional data set in healthcare, however, is clinical data within the EHR. The collection, standardization, and integration of these three types of data about individuals is the holy grail of personalized care and appropriately timed interventions, which should be optimized with integrated data.

The problem is that much of that data is siloed—silos of legacy data and silos of new data. The cloud driven by easy-to-use services spawned at a high rate by CSPs, makes it difficult to develop a single data platform capable of consuming, storing, and providing secure and authorized access for data scientists.

Over the medium to long term, as the healthcare industry demands easier access to data and more consistent data standards, unified, open data platforms will develop. These data platforms will be cloud-based, will leverage open source standards such as FHIR, and be easy for developers to use. These data platforms, and the myriad of read and write connections they will support, will have to enforce consistent compliance configurations. Additionally, they will have to maintain tens, if not hundreds of data connections.

Legacy to digital in all industries

An effective data integration strategy is required to succeed on the cloud regardless of industry. The cloud is being adopted in bits and pieces. This is happening directly and through vendors and partners, so an integration strategy to connect data is essential. This chapter delves deeply into healthcare integration and the major legacy systems that currently serve the EHRs. In other industries, the legacy systems and digital tools will be different. However, data integration, and the importance of including it in a cloud compliance strategy, is equally imperative.

Managing a Managed Service

Diving into a specific example highlights both the challenge and best solution to meeting compliance of a given service. Identify the depth, inventory all controls, then rinse and repeat across all other components of the cloud architecture.

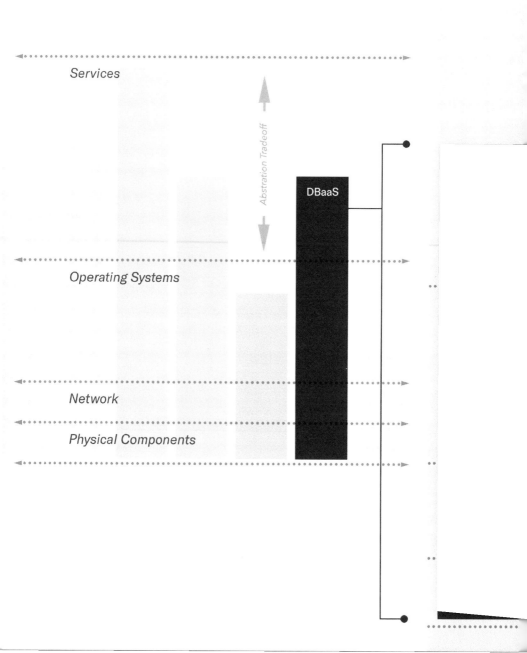

Services

Abstraction Tradeoff

DBaaS

Operating Systems

Network

Physical Components

Administrative Policies &
Procedures specific to
this given DBaaS service

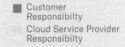

Customer
Responsibilty

Cloud Service Provider
Responsibilty

Example of Database as a Service

Users have access to a database via APIs, but don't
have to worry about managing versions, volumes,
performance, scalability, redundancy, backups, or other
common database headaches.

*Options include: Azure SQL Database, AWS RDS,
Google Cloud SQL, MongoDB Atlas, Azure CosmosDB,
AWS Dynamo DB, Google Cloud Datastore, and many
more.*

At the top of the stack, a DBaaS **service** typically offers slightly
less abstraction and slightly more control than a service like
serverless computing, for example. However, typically only a
handful of controls at this layer will be covered by a DBaaS
service, which means customers must account for the gap and
hope the service provides the ability to do it themselves.

OS controls are hard to configure and hard to manage, but
completely the responsibility of the customer. Some will be
taken care of by the DBaaS service, but sometimes they aren't
covered by the service. It's up to the customer to investigate if
they have the configuration ability to satisfy the control
themselves.

Network compliance controls are almost always handled by the
CSP, but here we start to see the splitting of shared
responsibility because a CSP might not take on some duties,
like TLS termination on the CSP loadbalancers. It is up to the
user to investigate where their liabilities lie.

CSPs handle all **physical components** of the cloud, and
thankfully take on all risks and responsibilities associated to the
physical layer. Users needn't worry about controls at this layer.

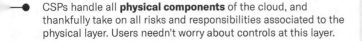

CHAPTER 5

Complete Cloud Compliance

Compliance is a top priority and executive-level initiative at all large enterprises because it essentially minimizes liability for all things data and technology. For highly-regulated industries like healthcare and finance, this has always been the case. Yet, recent trends like GDPR burden almost every company that stores personally identifiable information (PII), like protected health information (PHI) in healthcare, with the need to understand and attest to different compliance regimes.

When it comes to liability exposed by regulations, organizations are only as strong as the weakest component in their privacy, security, and compliance programs. Compliance, in its breadth, is based on the principle of weak links. The smartest organizations employ a strategy that mitigates low-hanging security fruit, so to speak, and not one that strengthens the already strong links. Over-optimization can be a killer.

The cloud is also becoming a first-class citizen for every entity, from enterprises to startups. The cloud, as defined in the previous chapter, fundamentally changes the required approach for compliance. For the first time, the cloud has split IT hardware and software resources into a myriad of primitives, or software-accessible services, that are consumed on an as-needed basis with almost infinite elasticity. Cloud primitives are redefining the technology stack as resources offered in layers, or levels of abstraction managed and controlled by third-party vendors, that have never been available before.

Weak links break the chain

The weakest link within a cloud environment defines the level of liability borne by the cloud infrastructure owner. Think about it: within the world of HIPAA, if proper encryption is set to meet rule §164.312(e)(1) but proper access controls aren't in place to meet rule §164.312(c)(1), then it doesn't matter how good the encryption, the cloud environment as a whole is not compliant for the parts owned by the organization as defined in a business associate agreement. In this case, the weak link is improper access controls which expose the entire cloud environment, and, by extension, the entire organization that owns the cloud environment, to the liability of a security incident data breach or the PR disaster of a data breach.

The 2013 Target data breach of personal and financial information tells the story of weak links in security. In this case, malicious hackers accessed sensitive Target customer information by gaining access through an unlikely partner, an HVAC vendor. It didn't matter that Target had secured its own systems or that it had completed PCI audits. Target had provided a business partner with external network access, costing the company $10 million in the end. This public and expensive breach highlights the differences between security and compliance, and the challenges associated with securing all the links in the technology chain[31].

An imperative for remaining competitive in every market today, organizations must leverage the cloud and must achieve *Complete Cloud Compliance*, or *3C* for short, which is a program designed to address all liability gaps exhibited by the cloud.

Achieving complete compliance **of**, **on**, and **in** the cloud means eliminating weak links in the chain of cloud workloads. The abstraction of the cloud creates many new third-party links via managed services. Employing a *3C* program dynamically addresses the compliance implications of each of those new cloud services links. The best approach is to think in multiple dimensions: both depth and breadth of compliance coverage are required for modern compliance management programs to minimize the risk of incidents or the liability of breaches across abstractions.

Abstraction creates many more links to manage

The cloud is not simply somebody else's computer, or a computer physically located in a facility owned and operated by a data center provider. The cloud now includes software-accessible services that enable specific, increasingly discrete, tasks that empower simple-to-use functionality. Prior to the introduction of the cloud, configuration and management of all layers of computer servers were required, from the physical hardware to networking, as well as the operating system up through software packages installed on the underlying OS.

The move to greater cloud abstraction mandates moving beyond a reliance on a CSP for physical security.

Abstraction on the cloud is tied directly to the concept of Shared Responsibility. While a helpful mental model, diving into what that means within the definition of abstraction is a good way to understand *Complete Cloud Compliance.*

The value of (and confusion around) abstraction

Technological abstractions, in their simplest form, are layers of the technology stack that have been removed from the management of the users of those services. Abstraction is a well-established method in computer science for removing certain details to enable focus on other areas of interest. Abstractions created by CSP managed services remove layers of technology that are necessary for creating and maintaining a certain experience, but, in terms of the direct use of the service, are not relevant to the customer. This is where the "managed" part of "managed services" comes in.

Abstraction jumpstarted innovation around economies of scale, which has been a major driver of modern technological advancement. But the issue with abstraction is its relationship to security and compliance, which must be "full stack" in order to be complete. All parties subject to compliance regimes, like GDPR, must ensure every layer of the technology stack is secured with liability properly outlined. In the cloud world abstraction makes this nearly impossible.

The most common example of abstracted cloud services today are managed databases, or DBaaS, like AWS Relational Database Service (RDS), Azure SQL Database, Google Cloud SQL, or MongoDB Atlas. Managed databases offer pre-built, configurable database instances with built-in redundancy, read and write optimization, scaling, and better performance than most organizations could achieve themselves. Managed services like DBaaS change IT staffing too; gone are the days of contacting the local database administrator to set up and manage a database or a local security officer to verify security configurations.

While managed services, like DBaaS, are simple and powerful in their easy-to-consume design, their black box nature is a prime example of the compliance conflict currently present on the cloud.

During an interview with the popular podcast *Software Engineering Daily*[32], in response to why Box chose to run its own Kubernetes cluster and not use a managed Kubernetes service from a CSP, Sam Ghods, co-founder and vice-president of technology, said, "We have to chip away at it piece-by-piece because we have strict compliance requirements around what runs on our servers, what software packages are running and how they are configured that support our code. So, we can't say, 'Well, just give us an image that works, and we'll be good with that.' We have patching requirements and configuration requirements for the kind of workloads that we run."

Sam understands the compliance tradeoffs of abstraction. In order for Box to meet the compliance requirements of its highly-regulated customers, Sam and his team needed to control certain parts of Kubernetes that were abstracted away from CSP managed services, like AWS EKS, Azure AKS, and GCP GKE. Not to mention at the time of that interview, some of those managed Kubernetes services weren't available, and none were backed by the CSP business associate agreement.

With more abstraction, more responsibility resides with the owner of the managed service since the customer doesn't have as much control by nature of what is abstracted away. Using DBaaS, again: Some compliance requirements, like encryption, might be the responsibility of the managed service provider because the customer may not have the capability to properly configure and monitor encryption. In some cases, like encryption, the responsibility may reside with the CSP customer, but the actual configuration is often done by a developer, not an information security specialist, as has traditionally been the case. Some of the power and value of managed cloud services is the ease of use, opening up new personnel to security and compliance responsibilities.

Each layer of abstraction is a link in the chain of security, compliance, and liability. Applying the concept of weak links within the model of Shared Responsibility, organizations must ensure that every link, or every layer of abstraction for a managed service like DBaaS, is secured and does not expose that organization to undue risk. If a CSP makes a mistake in any layer, like the HVAC vendor in the Target breach referenced above, the integrity of the entire cloud environment is at risk.

The evolution of cloud compliance with managed services

You can track the changes in compliance on the cloud by following the changes to privacy agreements such as business associates agreements (BAAs). In the not too distant past, back in 2013 when the HIPAA Omnibus Rule went into effect and created a category of entities called Subcontractors, HIPAA became relevant to the CSPs and offering BAAs for cloud services became a require-ment to sell into healthcare.

AWS was the first CSP to offer BAAs to customers in the fall on 2013. The BAA was under NDA but one of the public requirements for AWS to sign a BAA was that customers had to run what are dedicated instances. These are dedicated AWS EC2 instances with hardware dedicated to the customer and not shared. Dedicated instances are expensive and cost almost $1,400 per month per AWS region.

This paradigm of dedicated instances was clearly tied to the cloud hardware paradigm when you could dedicate hardware to a specific customer. Dedicated hardware is not an option with managed services, which is why AWS stopped requiring dedicated instances to sign BAAs in 2016. Managed services run on fleets of hardware shared by managed services customers.

The shift from dedicated, single tenant hardware to shared, multi-tenant managed services is reflective of how far the cloud and CSPs have come in a short time. It also clearly demonstrates how quickly technology is moving and how approaches to compliance in a post-cloud world must move equally fast.

The breadth and depth of compliance

The cloud exposes emergent discrete services as software, not hardware, and that software is consumed on demand to virtual endless scale. The CSPs race to offer expanded services that organizations consume to solve business and technical needs. The names and acronyms are hard to remember, let alone the security and compliance implications of each.

Managed databases are a small sampling of abstracted services available for cloud-native architectures. Managed services are available for everything from big data and container orchestration to machine learning and artificial intelligence, with CSPs adding new services at a pace of almost one per week. Modern developers are adopting the new CSP services almost as fast as they are launched, with regulated industries lagging behind, or worse, potentially unaware of the managed services being used by their IT groups and developers. The only way for regulated industries to keep pace is to ensure the configuration of all CSP services meets compliance requirements on a continuous basis.

The cloud, and the breadth of managed CSP services, makes even basic compliance functions more difficult. For example, external audits and internal risk assessments require an inventory of IT systems and services, documented networks, and storage destinations. The cloud has made this a much more dynamic and difficult process. The cloud has even changed the data that needs to be collected, or that can be collected. Oftentimes, the audit templates for IT inventory mandates the collection of certain data such as hardware SKU numbers or information about the operating system and disparate software versions, which is typically not available for the hardware and software underlying CSP managed services. A few simple examples: AWS customers cannot ask AWS for SKU numbers for the servers running the RDS software they use; Azure customers cannot inventory the software installed on servers running serverless compute tasks; customers running machine learning algorithms on Google Cloud hardware cannot request state information of the hardware. This is what Sam Ghods referenced earlier.

To complicate matters more, some CSP services are covered by data privacy agreements, such as business associate agreements for HIPAA and data processing agreements for GDPR, and some are not. The list of services covered by privacy agreements is constantly changing. It's hard enough for an internal auditor or compliance officer to keep track; it's not realistic to expect developers and cloud end users to stay current and ensure the services they use are compliant.

With more architectures becoming cloud-native, adoption of managed services—and consequently abstraction—is increasing, which poses a challenge for a *3C* program due to misaligned legal practices.

As one can imagine, compliance programs and liability agreements have not kept pace with the rapid innovation of cloud services. Take AWS for example: The number of AWS services included in the company's BAA, like RDS or serverless computing, has always been a smaller subset of the total number of AWS services available thus limiting compliant options for healthcare customers[33]. This is no one's fault, but simply the natural process of compliance catching up to technological innovation. It's the same scenario found at Microsoft Azure, Google Cloud Platform, and other cloud-based platform or service providers.

Actively developing and updating a list of approved cloud services is essential for every enterprise, as is an inventory of all services in use governed by privacy agreements. The challenge with this essential compliance task is that the inventory list will be highly dynamic, requiring employees or trusted third parties skilled in cloud-native technologies.

As architectures move from monolithic to microservice-based, the breadth of compliance concerns expands rapidly.

Developer control and risk

One reason breadth is getting out of hand is that CSPs and microservice solution providers have made everything so darn easy to use, which, to be clear, is a wonderful design achievement to be celebrated. Developers can now easily turn on and off functions, like Docker containers or DBaaS, without needing to configure servers or networks. With varying layers of abstraction, developers have the ability to set configurations. Many of those configurations are security-specific, such as encryption or access controls. This opens the door to an entirely new problem for enterprises leveraging the cloud.

Historically, IT would provision servers and software for developers, and security or compliance would sign-off before the use of those resources. Now, with the ease of the cloud and the shifting paradigm to developer empowerment, software developers are able to provision, configure, and use technology themselves, typically in the form of managed services from CSPs.

Expecting developers to stay abreast of both the available managed services and the security and compliance implications of those services is unrealistic.

Data integration: the new, crucial link

Interoperable infrastructure is a prerequisite for interoperable data, which is what leads to a unified view of disparate data sources. This matters because locked-up data is increasingly useless. One way to interpret healthcare's terrible interoperability record is by examining how woefully behind the industry is with API-driven and microservices-based cloud architectures.

Now, data integration on the cloud is more complicated than on-premises integrations because, by nature, the data is flowing in and across shared resources and networks. The increase of integrations inherently increases compliance breadth as well.

Considering the additional risk of data access, mitigating that risk cannot be accomplished without proper security. Also, the fragmented nature of digital applications and the lack of standardization on cloud and data platforms means that no decent market solutions exist to solve the problem. Successful strategies require flexible data integration tools that support different forms of data access.

Simply knowing the breadth is inadequate. Each managed service offers some amount of abstraction from the underlying hardware, network, and software. Things get even more difficult when trying to address the *depth* of the *breadth*.

The challenge of compliance for abstraction on the cloud is nontrivial in its complexity. The variability of depth per each managed or microservice in the breadth of an environment must be reworked for each geographic compliance regime the organization plans to prove.

Containers on the rise

Container services, specifically managed container services on a CSP, are an excellent illustration of abstraction variability impacting compliance. Take AWS as an example. As of July 2018, AWS offers two primary container services, an Elastic Container Service (Amazon ECS) and an Elastic Container Service for Kubernetes (Amazon EKS). Setting up a managed cluster of Docker containers is made easier with these services. The major component of a container service is orchestration, or the function of deploying and managing containers across a fleet of hosts or virtual machines (VMs). Amazon ECS uses an AWS-developed container orchestration software. Amazon EKS uses an open source orchestration software developed by Google, called Kubernetes. In the case of Amazon ECS, AWS manages its own orchestration system for customers. In the case of Amazon EKS, AWS manages Kubernetes for customers. Amazon ECS and Amazon EKS customers have less control over orchestration, aside from a few configuration settings, which is a good thing.

To underscore why this seemingly simple example matters, let's talk about the authors' recent experience securing Kubernetes for HITRUST CSF Certification. Datica developed a container orchestration platform in 2013 because we concluded that the available orchestration tools at the time were not mature enough for use in production. In 2018, we switched to utilizing Kubernetes for orchestration as it had matured to a point of stability that we felt it was ready for production, but, in order to comply with our policies and pass our same annual audits, we had to heavily modify the open source version of Kubernetes to enhance encryption support. Without that fix, any Kubernetes cluster was effectively operating out of compliance with our policies and, ultimately HITRUST, meaning we couldn't rely on one of the three CSP managed Kubernetes services to be our backbone for product delivery because it wasn't possible for us to have control at that level unless we built the cluster ourselves.

The complexity of depth of compliance with container services doesn't end with orchestration. To make the container services more complicated from a compliance standpoint, AWS offers two different modes for Amazon ECS and Amazon EKS—Fargate launch type and Amazon Elastic Compute Cloud (Amazon EC2) launch type. With Fargate, AWS manages all underlying servers and cluster configurations. With EC2 launch type, the AWS customer manages the underlying services on which the cluster runs. According to the AWS Fargate site , "EC2 launch type gives you more control of your server clusters and provides a broader range of customization options, which might be required to support some specific applications or possible compliance and government requirements."[34]

One additional data point: Initially the AWS BAA covered Fargate, but only for Amazon ECS. Only recently in 2018 did AWS cover Fargate for Amazon EKS under its BAA.

Considering the nuance found with containers and obtaining full compliance, the following questions may arise:

- How does a developer choose a container service that aligns with the compliance requirements of his or her company?
- How does a compliance officer understand the implications of these different layers of abstraction?
- How does an auditor verify all layers of the technology stack comply with an organization's policies and procedures?

Ultimately, CSPs must address the liability for each layer of abstraction across all services in order to spur consumption from regulated industries. Since different CSP services have multiple layers of abstraction, different services have varying Shared Responsibility profiles, meaning different responsibilities that can be shared with a CSP is variable by the cloud services. CSP customers must actively manage these dynamic Shared Responsibility profiles with CSPs.

Full-breadth + Full-depth = *Complete Cloud Compliance*

When it comes to compliance, a company is only as strong as its weakest link. When it comes to the cloud, more links are found in the technology stack than ever before because breadth is expanding, and depth is variable.

With the proliferation of CSP services, organizations moving to the cloud must adopt a system of *3C*. This means addressing, both on day zero and on an ongoing basis, the breadth of services used and the depth of abstraction and liability. To stay current, organizations must implement robust review and acceptance processes for new services. Compliance needs to be a key part of this review. Only by adopting privacy, security, and compliance by design can organizations ensure complete cloud compliance.

What *Complete Cloud Compliance* looks like

The case is made: the cloud is essential for digital transformation, which is essential for organizations to remain viable. Unfortunately, nothing fully ties together the compliance considerations needed for the microservices-based architectures of this modern era. *Complete Cloud Compliance* is the new mandate for the cloud.

A *3C* program, like the technologies being developed for the cloud today, must be cloud native. Cloud-native technologies are built as distributed systems that leverage software and managed services, taking full advantage of the commoditized nature of the underlying hardware and networks of the CSPs. To turn existing monolithic applications into cloud-native applications, environments must be re-architected based on microservices. Similarly, an established compliance program created in a pre-cloud world needs to be re-architected to adapt to the cloud.

The re-architecture of a compliance program for the cloud can take several different forms. As yet, no one-size-fits-all for cloud compliance exists. Likewise, no one-size-fits-all for microservices spread across geographic regions exists either. But, several common components are necessary to achieve *Complete Cloud Compliance.* Those are outlined below.

Office of Cloud Compliance (OCC)

The OCC is a new organizational function. In time, as organizations move more workloads to the cloud, the scale and importance of the OCC will grow; but, for the immediate term, the OCC should act like a sibling, or in some cases a child, of the overall compliance office at an organization while organizations operate in a hybrid cloud environment.

The OCC can be represented by one person or a group of individuals, but in all cases should engage regularly with stakeholders across multiple functional areas, like IT, risk, legal, external audit, innovation, etc. Actual functional groups will vary based on the organization. The OCC, as a dedicated function, is an essential first step in meeting the complexity and dynamic nature of cloud service and compliance.

Establishing a OCC is not arduous—do not let a perfect end state be the enemy of a good start. An organization should source the founding member from the technical portions of its organization, especially someone with rich cloud-native expertise.

Define the flow of compliance

The functions of privacy, security, and compliance must be synchronized. But, the flow of a *3C* program is equally important to ensure its correct. The necessary flow is outlined below. Of note, this is a similar flow to what HITRUST uses to assess the maturity of each control within the HITRUST CSF and is based on a similar model to what Carnegie Mellon originally developed.

1. **Policy.** The first step requires the OCC to pull inputs from both security and privacy so that the highest level of organizational policies around technology and data are defined. These policies should consider both the principles of the organization with respect to data privacy, as well as the requirements of the compliance regimes to which the organization must comply.

2. **Procedure.** Once policies have been drafted and approved, they should be translated into actionable procedures. Prescriptive procedures are essential for ensuring policies are actionable and aligned with the highest-level objectives for compliance.

3. **Implementation.** Procedures should be followed to implementation of actual technology and practices. The implementation is the tactical manifestation of the policies themselves and the procedures are the crosswalk between the policies and the implementation.

4. **Monitor.** Implementation of controls and practices to comply with internal policies is not simply a day zero problem, just as compliance should not be seen as a "one and done", or snapshot, requirement. In any organization and environment, but especially so in an organization leveraging the cloud, continually monitoring the implementation of compliance policies becomes essential.

5. **Manage.** If properly monitored, procedures and resources need to be created and available to ensure issues that arise from monitoring are mitigated or, in some cases, documented as exceptions. A common term today is *continuous compliance*, which is something every cloud compliance program should attempt but can only be successful if compliance is a first-class citizen.

At the policy level, organizations should develop a data integrity policy. That policy should meet the requirements for data integrity of the desired compliance regimes and should be mapped to procedures for implementing specific controls for things like backup, redundancy, and service level agreements (SLAs). Taking backup as an example, those should be conducted nightly, as well as regularly monitored and tested to ensure backups can be used when necessary for data integrity requirements outlined in the policy.

If the above compliance flow is implemented and followed, security and compliance are in place by design.

The best compliance program design comes from a sequential process that builds upon itself. Adopting a similar flow ensures privacy and security are in place from the start.

Privacy agreement management

Third-party risk assessments, conducted annually, now demand more attention. In a cloud-native world where Shared Responsibility is the king, large entities rely on third parties to manage ever more parts of their technology infrastructure. Each entity is different, meaning each service varies in abstraction and responsibility.

Given the technical complexity of the cloud, a new approach is needed to assess the security and compliance programs and posture of cloud vendors. The existing tools, in the form of assessment questionnaires, fall short because they were not created to assess cloud vendors.

While some of the work required to ensure complete cloud compliance is technical, another key component is data privacy agreements. Data privacy agreements take different forms and have various names, but most are mandated by compliance regimes. In HIPAA, data privacy agreements are called business associate agreements but are sometimes referred to as business associate addendums by CSPs. In GDPR, they are so named, data privacy agreements. All are a necessary legal vehicles that outline responsibilities and liabilities for customers and vendors within each aspect of the provided service.

Traditionally, organizations used their own data privacy agreements with external partners and vendors. That model flipped with the introduction of hyperscale CSPs and cloud-based vendors.

Out-sized scale and subsequent leverage available to CSPs are used to standardize customers onto singular privacy agreements with terms dictated by the CSP, meaning organizations on the cloud must now assume the burden of:

- Aligning multiple privacy agreements across different languages, vocabulary definitions, formats, and locations.
- Mapping multiple privacy agreements to their own risk management and compliance programs.
- Developing management plans to mitigate liability gaps exposed in some privacy agreements but not others.

It doesn't become easier, especially considering the conditions required by privacy agreements, including how many from CSPs are kept under NDA, for example. The conditions have good business reasons, however, because along with hyperscale comes massive liability for the CSPs. Moreover, delivering the low-cost, customer-focused, scalable services that CSPs deliver today would be impossible if it weren't for those CSPs employing standardized privacy agreements with minimal liability claims. CSPs must limit their liability to adequately scale. The scale and liability of CSPs have upset the balance between service provider and customer.

Many industries, such as healthcare, have tried to create standardized privacy agreements; these efforts, sadly, have failed. Standardization would simplify end-user software agreements, but, while a noble goal, not enough interest has been expressed by regulated industries to make it a reality.

Given all of this, organizations must consider third-party risk and vendor assessments when planning a move to the cloud. The onus is on organizations to get it right or remain accountable for things that are out of their control. Too much complexity and liability exist. Not creating a robust, full-featured partner assessments program with a major focus on privacy agreements is ill-advised.

Approved cloud configurations

Managed services from cloud vendors make configuring, deploying, and scaling technology infrastructure easier for IT, both developers and operators. Instead of configuring operating systems, network parameters, and configuration files, customers are given configuration options as variables or service parameters they can set themselves. Setting these parameters by web interface or command line interface (CLI) is quite different from directly configuring and managing the layers, such as the operating system and database. Instead of having the parameters set and managed by UNIX administrators, database or network administrators, the cloud now enables software developers to set and manage these parameters.

For each cloud service, every parameter should have an approved setting that maps to the compliance policies of the organization that decides the approved security states for an organization's cloud services. Parameter settings can then be disseminated to all staff who interact with cloud vendors and do point-in-time audits of cloud services.

At times, certain parameters cannot be set or modified for a managed service, as with installed software packages or package versions. In those cases, services should not be approved for use by the organization.

Given the number of cloud services and associated parameters, this process of creating approved cloud configurations and states is quite easy to get wrong.

A few examples of RDS parameters are:

- Master Password
- Publicly Accessible (yes / no)
- Enable Encryption
- Database Port
- Backup Retention
- DB Version
- Many more

Dynamic, real-time visibility

Much of the OCC's effort is to ensure an organization's compliance posture adapts to the rapid and constantly changing cloud landscape. With the speed of the cloud, this is often near real-time. The days of being able to walk down to the basement data center once a quarter and inventory hardware SKU numbers rack to rack, or verify physical security and HVAC systems on site, or even to check OS versions or package install lists are gone. The requirements to gain and provide visibility into cloud resources require new knowledge, processes, and tools.

The first step is to inventory all cloud resources being operated by an organization. Not as easy as it seems for organizations that can have multiple functional groups managing cloud resources with different accounts and sub-accounts. Groups, if not otherwise restricted, will often use separate managed services provided by CSPs. Additionally, inventories should include relevant geographic information about the specific region in which the services are leveraged from the CSP.

Visibility is not simply an inventory of cloud services and privacy agreements, it's also the security states, or configurations, of those cloud services. Once the complete inventory of cloud resources, the state, or security state are in hand, all resources and environments must be documented. Almost every organization uses a manual process for documentation today. However, CSPs and cloud vendors are providing better, more real-time access to state information via APIs. In the future, the documentation process should be largely automated.

Therefore, inventory and state data need to be stored, along with metadata. Pulling the relevant information on an organization's cloud workloads doesn't go far enough. To prove continual compliance an organization must create a historical record of inventory and associated states at each point in time.

Additionally, the approved cloud states must be used to evaluate the technical security and compliance of third-party vendors and partners. As with privacy agreements, this is a different process than previously used for evaluating third-party vendors. As with the pace of the cloud and internal, organizational-owned technology on the cloud, technical evaluations of third parties must be done on a regular basis, ideally with the onus on partners and third parties.

Cloud compliance education

The modern cloud is new to everyone, even for technologists that adopted the cloud 10 years ago. Cloud technology is changing so rapidly that cloud veterans must constantly learn new ways to use it. Building an effective cloud compliance program is essentially about building cloud compliance capacity as a function within an organization. To do that, education is a cornerstone.

The security and compliance education available today doesn't address the cloud. The education is outdated. Even if up to date, the knowledge would be outdated in 12 months. Thus, one of the key compliance roles is to ensure relevant cloud education is provided to all workforce members that engage with the cloud. This is a growing list of functional groups from IT to innovation and from risk to legal, and operations.

Achieving *Complete Cloud Compliance*

The ensuing chapter outlines next steps for building a cloud compliance program. While the process may seem daunting, it will be easier today than in a year or two, or five, when playing catch-up.

The key is to build cloud compliance as a core competency within the organization as early as possible. It's a journey, not a one-and-done checklist, so reviewing the proven best practices for a *3C* program implementation in the next chapter is a critical place to begin.

CHAPTER 6

Best Practices for Complete Cloud Compliance

Compliance officers face two trends as outlined here: the increase in compliance regimes across the globe, and the acceleration of the cloud.

First, the compliance footprint, which can be thought of as a data liability portfolio, has broadened as enterprises have gone digital. Whether that's digitizing internal processes or instantiating new solutions, the footprint is larger than ever before.

The second trend is the movement to the cloud, which introduces a number of areas that lie outside of enterprise's control. This means more than an organization using someone else's computers to run its data. On the cloud, an organization can no longer control all the pieces it controlled in the past—the physical hardware, infrastructure, data centers, piping, power, and air conditioning.

But beyond that layer of machines in somebody else's data center lay software tools being managed and operated by the cloud service providers, who are chopping up all layers of the technology stack between the data center and users.

Compliance has not kept pace. How can one possibly keep up?

Employing a *Complete Cloud Compliance* program is one method. To date, the concept has proven useful for both startups and Fortune 100 enterprises. Now that the program is understood, moving on to proven best practices can provide an even clearer path toward compliance in the cloud.

Create a cloud compliance roadmap

If an organization has a cloud technology roadmap, then it should have a cloud compliance roadmap. The OCC should keep pace with an organization's cloud consumption. A compliance roadmap, linked to a broader organizational cloud roadmap, is a great way to align cloud compliance with the overall organizational goal.

The structure for the cloud compliance roadmap should include several key elements:

1. A risk assessment of the organization's current cloud footprint. The assessment doesn't have to be too deep but should give both a sense of the organization's scope of the data being stored or processed on the cloud, as well as the number of cloud providers the organization works with currently.

2. A detailed plan and timeline for how to either augment current organization cloud policies and procedures or develop completely new cloud policies and procedures.

3. A list of the relevant functional groups within the organization to work with on cloud compliance.

4. A rough organizational chart of the ways in which the OCC will interface with the rest of the organization.

5. A timeline of audits to include, or be exclusive to, the cloud.

Itemize the 'breadth' first, then the 'depth' of each item

No strategy exists without intelligence. The only way to deploy a *3C* program is to start by creating an inventory of the organization's entire cloud architecture.

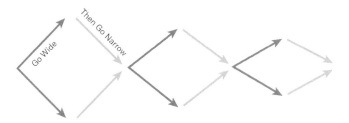

An excellent problem-solving approach is called "Source and Filter." The two-step process entails collecting a broad array of probable causes, symptoms, and characteristics of the problem, then filtering out unlikely causes to a small subset that can be worked to solve the problem. Try the pattern sometime and start using it in everyday work situations.

For managing compliance on the cloud, the pattern starts by itemizing the organization's entire compliance portfolio so that liabilities are evident. The process is tedious, but thankfully can have a repeatable approach.

First, document every cloud service within the organization's architecture. Make sure it's charted by entity, as well as offering and be sure to enumerate all services from a single entity. For example, if using AWS, be sure to list AWS EC2, AWS RDS, AWS S3, and so on. Itemize the common properties important to the service, like a BAA (HIPAA) or data processing agreement (DPA, GDPR) on file. Repeat across all services in the list.

An inventory of cloud workloads is consistently harder to create and maintain than an inventory of physical machines because it must include all cloud services, many of which are software-based. A shortcut for starting with an inventory is to leverage a cloud finance tool, such as Cloudability. Cloud financial management tools are often used by large organizations to predict and optimize their cloud spend and are utilized along the entire lifecycle of the cloud, from pre-planning migration to annual optimization. The OCC can piggyback on the early work of finance to quickly create a list of currently used services and even use financial data as a proxy for seeing cloud services growth at the organization.

At this point, split the list based on those that have a BAA or DPA, and those that don't. For the ones that don't, make a decision on the possibility of continued use of the service. However, utilizing those most likely won't be an option going forward.

For those selected for continual use, review the BAA or DPA on file. When complete, you should have a full understanding around the liability gaps, based on levels of abstraction and accountability outlined in privacy agreements, exposed to you per service.

Now, a data set that powers a *3C* program is in hand. Options for a corrective action are then possible for each service that exposes an abstracted liability, thus minimizing that accountability:

- Negotiate with the CSP to cover that liability in contracts. Note: this can be difficult if not impossible but has to be attempted. The attempts at negotiating these points should be documented and, at times, become compliance exceptions.

- Work with engineering to implement a programmable solution, then document that solution in organizational policies and procedures. This may only be available if the control is accessible. For example, with a DBaaS product, encryption may not be an option for usable control.

- Utilize UIs and APIs provided by the service to adjust configurations. This will help meet the controls required and is often the best approach. However, many services don't expose all configurations required via an interface and can be a challenge.

- Utilize additional software tools and managed services to monitor or configure those services.

Know the 'weak links' and optimize towards addressing them

After itemizing the entire landscape of your compliance obligations, identify the weakest links because those are the most urgent to address. Identifying the weak links is straightforward:

- First, any service which does not provide a BAA, DPA, or some other contract outlining risk ownership between the organization and the service is an immediate red flag and the weakest link. In many cases, it is a requirement: in healthcare, an organization must have a BAA with all service providers or risk noncompliance.

- For those left, consider where the service lies in the 'depth' of abstraction. The higher up the stack, the more controls the service must take on. Investigate if a highly-abstracted service, like emergent serverless computing, does everything required all the way down the entire stack. In general, the higher the abstract, the greater the probability of the service being a weak link.

- Across all services, but especially with the more abstracted options, the weakest links will be the services that do not provide compliance documentation or attestation.

- Those that do provide documentation may not provide configuration options. Those are the next weakest.

Pick one 'compliance DNA' and crosswalk that to other global regimes

Compliance officers have seen a number of entities put together big catalogs of controls. Some of the most common are ISO 27001, HITRUST, ITIL, and COBIT, to name a few.

Often, if not completely, those lists of controls are written with a different language and in a different order, but ultimately the lists say the same thing. As a result, that list of things that an organization should do is largely, if not completely, the same from one to the other.

Experienced organizations with mature compliance programs pick one compliance DNA, or regime, and then map it to other regimes. That is called a crosswalk, and several crosswalks between all of these different regimes exist already. With HITRUST, which has emerged as one of the better frameworks for this strategy, compliance officers find relative ease in mapping a HITRUST CSF control to specific ISO or NIST controls. In many ways, HITRUST was created explicitly to standardize those crosswalks.

"The HITRUST CSF was built with many compliance regimes in mind," said Michael Parisi, Vice President - Assurance Strategy and Community Development at HITRUST. "From when we started in 2007 to today, we found that cross walking our catalog of controls to other regulations across the globe grew as a primary feature of the CSF."

The process is simple:

1. Pick a root compliance framework. HITRUST CSF is suggested, but other options, like the ISO 27000 series or the NIST Special Publication 800-series risk management framework, can be chosen.

2. Do the basic work of mapping the technology, processes, procedures, and policies to the root framework.

3. Conduct a first audit in the main geography to ensure complete adherence to all framework requirements.

4. Select the next compliance regime depending on the organization's compliance or international growth priorities.

5. Map the root framework to the new regime. Include all technology, processes, and policies specific to that regime.

6. Conduct an audit against the new mappings in the new regime.

7. Rinse and repeat from step four.

While the format sounds trivial, few organizations employ this approach. Yet, it remains the best way to quickly deploy an airtight compliance program across many regimes and geographies.

Dynamic documentation

When changing anything from policies to procedures to actual cloud configuration, every change should be logged and the body of documentation should be retained. In an ideal world, this record of changes should include who initiated the change, the reasons for the change, and the approval of the change, along with all date information about the request and approval.

Leveraging a version control program or platform can automate much of the work of creating and maintaining documentation on compliance program and configuration changes. Two popular options are the commercial tool Github[35], as well as an open source, self-hosted option GitLab[36]. The trail of evidence makes external audits much more efficient.

Target risk assessments – assess risk in real time

Risk assessments are a key aspect of an effective compliance program, ideally as a part of a larger enterprise risk management (ERM) program. In traditional technology environments, assessments are performed annually or when significant technology changes occur. When leveraging the cloud, risk assessments should be done on a more regular cadence.

The most common form of risk assessment is based on NIST guidelines for risk assessments[37]. In the simplest terms, a risk assessment weighs the likelihood of different threats against an organization with the level of impact if those threats affect an organization. Based on those factors and weighting, most of which is highly subjective, a risk score, or more typically a rating, is calculated for each threat. Organizations should create plans to address all risks, and prioritize mitigation for those risks considered high or very high.

Risk assessments, in their traditional, static approach, have limited value on the cloud. Similar to any snapshot of the cloud, having a point in time assessment when a target, like the cloud, is constantly moving is of limited value. Targeted risk assessments must be dynamic when it comes to cloud workloads.

The framework used for monitoring continuous compliance should also include regular risk assessments. This can be daunting if the method used for risk assessments are static spreadsheets. Consider a model similar to the above referenced version control model to capture the change in risk associated with changes in cloud configurations and services.

Question all vendor claims

Be wary of service providers who claim to be "HIPAA Compliant" because, while it may be *true*, it's not always *truthful*. A strategy of *trust by verify* should be employed. Vendors may well be compliant at the layers they attest to in their BAA, like the physical layer, but the responsibility of the other abstracted layers are still borne by the customer.

Never assume at face value what a service provider touts—not even the biggest and most trustworthy cloud providers—because the nuance of cloud liability extends beyond website marketing copy.

Instead, do trust that what vendors say is indeed the truth for the abstraction levels that the service provider can control. Then, ask questions and investigate how much of a liability gap is left to cover.

Be more granular in approving cloud vendors

As CSPs break apart technology, a seemingly infinite number of abstracted services can be launched where the only constant is change. Some are spawned while others are sunsetted. This dynamic landscape requires a more granular approval process for cloud vendors and a more specific list for approved cloud services for an organization.

Approved cloud services should be at the most specific level. If Microsoft is an approved cloud vendor for an organization, then that organization then needs to create a list of approved Azure cloud services. Each cloud service has different compliance implications due to the varying breadth of abstraction, configuration options, and coverage under privacy agreements. Even in the case of container orchestration services, the specific flavor of container services and even launch modes for those services need to be evaluated and approved for use.

Create approved 'states' for each approved cloud service

The state of approved cloud services, or the parameters set for them, are the cloud architecture version of configuration management. The problem is configuration management policies and procedures were not written for the cloud and must be adapted to ensure they can be followed and enforced when using cloud services. Creating approved configurations, or states, for all approved cloud services is an onerous task. And it needs to have input from IT, security, risk, and compliance. The best approach is to treat policies and procedures for cloud service states like other policies and procedures but waterfall down from approved CSP to approved CSP services, and then to approved states for each service.

Consolidate BAAs/DPAs to control the portfolio

Compliance officers, whether for their own technology or a third-party technology, are constantly inundated with data privacy agreements, and unfortunately no standard format exists.

Frameworks like HITRUST help but they aren't a panacea.

The lack of standardization at the contract level necessitates extraordinary overhead simply to review and align ongoing contractual agreements. The smaller the company, the harder and more expensive portfolio alignment becomes.

The lack of standardization is also a pain acutely felt within company policies because organizations must create internal policies per regime. Policies typically require third-party vendor due diligence, which is a core part of a risk management process. The traditional method is to send third-party vendors a list of questions involving information security and compliance-related controls. Companies also have the contract right to go onsite and look at the data center or walk through the server room. In the HIPAA world, a business associate agreement outlines that contractual agreement.

What's more likely to happen with customers or with companies conducting this third-party vendor diligence work is a strong need to have a person or several people on staff to handle these incoming and outgoing questionnaires. This becomes a significant cost center for the organization.

Don't get stuck in this pattern.

A better approach starts by consolidating contractual agreements, like BAAs within HIPAA or DPAs within GDPR. With fewer BAAs in place, for example, fewer misalignments or gaps occur.

Certainly, consolidation goes beyond BAAs or DPAs. Also consider consolidating the number of partners and vendors to engage. Fewer cloud-enabled managed services from different entities will make worldwide compliance management much easier from the outset.

Draft policies within regimes that are cloud native

A major part of any compliance program is the administrative policies an organization adopts to govern its employees, procedures, and the business itself. These policies need to be standardized for an organization and then cross-walked to the various compliance regimes to which the organization must comply. Ideally, the anchoring compliance regime chosen should map to other regimes.

Typical Audit Workflow

Risk Assessment

1

The anchoring audit step for an effective compliance program in general. Involves going through a questionnaire or framework and replying with risk, likelihood, impact, remediation values. Drives the overall risk profile and the rest of the activities or steps of the audit.

✓ *Completed Risk Assessment Questionnaire*

Penetration test

3

Systems are accessed and attempts are made to gain unauthorized access. Should be done by a 3rd party but some companies do them internally. Many levels of pen testing, but cloud compliance should focus on an external pen test.

✓ *Pen Test Report*

Evidence-Gathering

5

Auditors will ask for proof of processes and settings of systems, which will require chasing down data and documents. The most sophisticated companies keep an up-to-date "Audit Room" with all of this evidence up to date. It's ongoing work but always ready.

✓ *Audit Room*

Policy Review

2

An annual review of written policies. Involves evaluating policies to ensure they are up to date and adhered. Typically there are changes needed to remain up to date. These changes must be tracked and documented as to what changes were made and the justification.

✓ *Documentation of Review*

Network Architecture Diagram

4

Ideally, dynamic and simple on an ongoing basis.

Feeds inventory and geography tasks.

✓ *Complete Network Diagram*

Policy Review 7

An annual review of written policies. Involves evaluating policies to ensure they are up to date and adhered. Typically there are changes needed to remain up to date. These changes must be tracked and documented as to what changes were made and the justification.

✓ *Documentation of Review*

System/Data Inventory 9

All hardware and software systems used must be documented with their function and location.

✓ *System Information Spreadsheet*

3rd Party Assessment 10

All 3rd parties (e.g. partners, business associates, data processers, APIs, etc.) must have their contracts and privacy agreements reviewed each year. Must be documented along with a complete list of 3rd parties.

✓ *Proof of 3rd party review*

On-site Interviews 6

All real audits involve on-site interviews to review documentation with staff, learn more about the company, and generally launch the audit as a project. On-site interviews are potentially the most important part of the process as it's where the majority of the work is completed with the external third party who will independently validate your compliance posture.

✓ *Interview documentation as part of the audit report*

Geographic Reach 8

Must ensure clear agreements, processes, and documentation in place for the geographies with exposed liability of data loss.

✓ *Spreadsheet outlining all geographies that generate or consume data*

Not all policies are created equal, unfortunately. Organizations that use outdated policies, written during a pre-internet era, and have updated them to include sporadic cloud language are doing the organization a disservice. The result is not pretty, as those organizations only create more problems by often injecting unnecessary bureaucracy or accidentally leaving liability gaps within the language.

Adopting policies that are built from the ground up with cloud-native architectures in mind is the best way to make the administrative side of compliance work for a *3C* management program.

Don't be intimidated by this advice. Much of the work is already complete using several open source projects. Datica has open sourced its internal company policies for HIPAA, GDPR, and GxP under a Creative Commons license. Those policies are free to review, download, and mold into the right fit for any organization. Hundreds of organizations have adopted these open-sourced policies since being launched in January 2015.

Datica's Open Source Policies

In an effort to make compliance as easy as possible for digital companies working with PHI, Datica open sourced its policies. These policies were written with modern, cloud-based technology vendors in mind. Most importantly, these policies have been several extensive third-party HIPAA audits HITRUST CSF Certified assessments. Visit **datica.com**.

Adhere to the dynamic nature of the cloud

The cloud is moving fast. The services launched are changing, and services offered today are abstractions of technologies. Four to five years ago, services like Kubernetes didn't even exist. The way services are offered, and how the layers of abstraction and liability are managed, also have changed. Kubernetes or serverless computing are good examples of this. The dynamic nature of the cloud, and the inability to predict what cloud services will be available in the future, require a compliance DNA and approach to complete cloud compliance that is equally dynamic.

This isn't a throw-away point, either. Since 2016, an astounding number of Fortune 500 enterprises has told the authors that the dynamic, rapid pace of service innovation on the cloud is actually preventing cloud adoption. The irony is that due to the multi-month bureaucratic process of security and compliance review, once a new service or vendor is approved, the enterprise becomes worried that something better is available.

Don't get stuck in that situation. Design and operationalize a *3C* program to move as fast as the cloud does.

Treat developers as partners, not adversaries

The cloud enables software developers to deploy and manage infrastructure for their own application environments, which can massively accelerate the development and deployment time for new digital products and initiatives. However, this time escalation can also expose the organization to significant risk in the form of misconfigured technology. If not managed properly, this can remove IT and security from the process of configuring and approving technology before it goes to production.

Do not resist the cloud because it is all too easy for software developers to use it for themselves and configure incorrectly. The best approach for leveraging the cloud is to engage with developers to ensure configurations are approved when deploying new cloud services. The parameters for cloud services are easy to configure. That's why software developers have such an easy time operating cloud workloads and why shadow IT is enabled by the cloud. Developers simply need to have proper guidance and documentation to do it right.

Developer education should focus on two key areas. First, educate developers about cloud compliance, in general. Remember from the last chapter: education is a key part of complete cloud compliance. Second, educate specifically about approved cloud services and approved cloud states, or configurations.

Hire a data engineer

Monitoring any compliance program requires considerable amount of data reporting and storage. In the case of a cloud environment, the data requirements for compliance are even greater because of the myriad of services and the dynamic nature of cloud services. But, the cloud also exposes data about technology infrastructure and services that is easy to consume and use to optimize cloud operations and ensure continued compliance. Data on cloud services and configurations are readily available via APIs from all the major CSPs. The data today is still limited, and not all relevant compliance data is available via API, but this is changing.

For organizations to automate data reporting and trigger compliance alerts, a dedicated data function is necessary. This new role in compliance will be increasingly important.

The function of data engineering in compliance should include a data acquisition strategy, data mapping and structure, storage and retention, and exposure/querying. If done properly, and integrated deeply with a cloud compliance program, data engineering can streamline compliance, as well as IT audit functions.

Secure by design

The savviest organizations will build in the concept of "security by design," a practice now mandated in Europe via GDPR. This term means an organization must start from a "zero trust" position: no one is trustworthy along the entire link of the chain.

Mature organizations employ information security architects who participate in every IT project from kick-off to completion. Information security is a core part of the requirements gathering phase of a software project, but the level of involvement is contextual to the project. Sometimes information security architects are deeply involved with high-risk projects; at other times, they check in periodically during a phase like quality assurance testing.

Organizations build security into architectures from the start, instead of trying to bolt it on after the fact. If a project is secure by design, then it ends up being compliant by default. If work proceeds according to information security best practices, then that will dovetail with controls that are in alignment with compliance regimes. That's the ideal state for a mature organization.

Be prescriptive with compliance and flexible with security

The success of the cloud, and a big reason why developers have chosen to use it, is due to its flexibility. Organizations can choose the services wanted and easily configure them the way they are needed. Large or small organizations can choose the geography, the backup frequency, the open ports, the types of logs, and a slew of other parameters that can vary in terms of availability based on the specific cloud service. Flexibility makes the cloud powerful for users.

However, flexibility doesn't align well with compliance. Compliance is anchored in doing things in a documented, repeatable way with proof. When developers manage cloud workloads for organizations, whether those developers are employees or third parties, they must manage them with repeatable procedures approved by the organization.

This process of repeatability and proof ties directly to creating approved cloud states, or configurations, for services. The top-level compliance DNA, in the form of policies and procedures, must also be cross walked down to each cloud service so that the plethora of security parameter options for all cloud services are set in a prescriptive way. If done correctly, the flexibility of the cloud is retained but it is applied in a prescriptive way.

Treat compliance like a team sport

Compliance is not solely the domain of internal audit or privacy groups, or whatever other groups may have historically owned it. In this post-cloud world, with abstracted managed services from CSPs, the barriers between privacy, security (or info sec), and compliance have blended. And not just between those groups but also with IT. And, to complicate things further and necessitate more change in the way organizations view and operate their compliance programs, even within IT the barriers have been broken down and the cloud has enabled software developers to configure and deploy infrastructure without system admins or DBAs and, in many cases, without the explicit sign-off of security. In this brave new world of compliance on the cloud, operating compliance as a team sport is essential.

The cloud turns developers into admins

Managed services on the cloud, such as database-as-a-service (DBaaS), make it simple for software developers to deploy and scale their own infrastructure. Using web UIs or basic command line tooling and APIs, these managed services expose infrastructure pre-built for developers to use. The underlying layers of the technology stack have been abstracted away from users.

The setup of these services does not require a Linux or Windows admin meaning developers can now easily circumvent the process by setting up their own cloud services. Using the above referenced UIs, developers are essentially configuring parts of the underlying operating system, software packages, and networking. These configurations, if not set properly, can violate the policies of an organization and expose data to unauthorized access.

The operator construct must have security as a pillar

While empowering developers to directly interact with and manage their own infrastructure, the cloud does not remove the need for operations, it just changes the role and specific functions required of them. Managing large-scale cloud deployments required dedicated operators, not just developers. Setting up and managing development pipelines to the cloud is similarly the purview of operations and not developers. There are other examples of the new role DevOps plays on the cloud.

One area that is sometimes missed, but is becoming its own dedicated area, is SecDevOps, or security-focused DevOps. This is different from DevSecOps, which is the act of applying DevOps concepts to security management. Don't worry, it's confusing. The key thing to understand is security needs to be a core part of the function of DevOps on the cloud, whether for cloud workloads managed by operations or for simpler cloud workloads managed directly by developers. Operations groups need to work with compliance to translate existing policy and procedure requirements for the cloud to ensure whatever groups and individuals are managing cloud workloads are not exposing an entity to risk.

Compliance must inform the security posture operators enforce

Policies and procedures should be developed by compliance with input from privacy. Typically, the challenge on the cloud is the translation of these often static policies into more dynamic procedures and cloud configurations to meet the needs of IT to leverage new cloud services. This translation process is exceptionally difficult because it's a continual process to map compliance policies to new and emerging cloud services and configuration options. Compliance needs to work with operations, DevOps, or SecDevOps, to ensure the proper translation is created and maintained.

Internal audit and compliance must have visibility into cloud configs

Once approved cloud configurations have been established, visibility into deployed cloud workloads and actual configurations is required to ensure identification and remediation of gaps. Given the dynamic nature of the cloud and cloud services, gaps will emerge, necessitating near real-time visibility into the compliance posture of the cloud. The key to managing an effective compliance program on the cloud is transparency into cloud inventory (workloads, services, environments, etc.) and, ideally, proactive identification of gaps between approved cloud service configurations/states and actual cloud service configurations/states. The first step to remediate gaps is to identify them.

Education and alignment top-to-bottom is necessary

Compliance on the cloud is new but it is emerging, along with cybersecurity, as a top challenge for all organizations. The change now is that the only way to create and maintain a successful cloud compliance program is to align resources across multiple groups within an organization. From policy to cloud configurations to reporting and visibility, groups need to work together like links in a chain.

In many ways, compliance on the cloud is like an assembly line. Compliance, with input from privacy, designs the process, works with security and IT to implement it on the cloud, and creates real-time reporting to measure the outputs of the process. The only way for this to work is to operate as a team with a common goal—protect data and digital assets while enabling organizations to build the technology to continue to compete.

Operationalize the typical audit process

Organizations find the audit process debilitating until the first one is complete. Paralysis analysis crops up from a lack of understanding of the related time and costs involved.

Fear not, as the process is much more regular than one would think.

The audit process starts with a risk assessment that drives the overall risk profile. This informs the rest of the audit process. From there, a multi-week process ensues, involving policy review, penetration testing, and architecture documentation. This culminates in potentially the most important part of the process, which is the on-site interview with an auditor. After several weeks of interviews, the process is completed with more documentation and inventory. The definition of "done" is when the audit documentation has been received from the auditor that the process is now complete.

The audit process can take as long as four months or as short as 60 days. Sometimes audits can be expensive, sometimes cheap, but are always varied because cost is a combination of direct costs associated to an auditor's time or a penetration test, and indirect costs, like an organization's time away from building its business. Median audit costs fall into these ranges:

- HIPAA Gap Assessment - $17,800-$22,800
- Full HIPAA Audit - $27,000-$32,000
- Validated HITRUST Assessment - $44,000-$59,000[38]

The costliest aspect of an audit is time, to which the priciest action is being unprepared. If an organization operationalizes its audit, plans for the sequential phases, and works with an auditor as a partner, the process can likely be cut to about two months with a lower overall total cost.

The Achievable Mandate

Why does all this matter? Why do business professionals in regulated industries need to wrap their heads around controlling cloud compliance?

At its most basic, disruption brought on by the cloud is inevitable. The institutional change accelerated by the cloud will hit regulated industries too, and it will happen sooner rather than later. If companies don't react, they will be upended like other industries before them.

Reacting starts with changing mindsets.

The cloud today isn't someone else's data center, computer or hard drive anymore. That's thinking from twenty, fifteen, or even ten years ago. The cloud is now mostly about software-enabled services sitting on top of commodified hardware. Every enterprise that is going to remain viable in the future state of any industry must leverage interoperable software and data found on interoperable infrastructure, meaning digital transformation is now required as a core competency. The IT department cannot treat the cloud as a cost center off in the corner. The cloud needs to be a strategic asset of the business. To be fully leveraged, the strategy must take advantage of managed services provided by CSPs and other solution providers.

Companies are not going to build out their own solutions to run in co-located facilities, and those that do will fail. Organizations will leverage the CSPs as partners and get out of the IT hardware and data center management business, which no longer provides a competitive advantage. The cloud enables that transformation to happen, and at breakneck speed, because managed software services have become so modular and easy to integrate.

The challenge is in reframing IT resources from hardware to software components that can be stitched together. This has sparked a fundamental shift in the security and the compliance of the cloud.

When the cloud was about hardware on someone else's computer, security meant things like redundant power and cooling systems, whether they had retinal scanners or fingerprint scanners, and conducting background checks on all personnel.

Today, that's still a part of security, but security and compliance involve all of the pieces between the hardware and the software service being exposed—everything from the networking pieces to the firewalls, routers, load balancers, encryption, and the operating system. How are all the software packages being installed? How is the security of those packages managed? How are those resources shared across multiple customers?

These questions have significant implications for anyone in a regulated industry. Organizations will either rewrite or adjust some requirements when it comes to things like packages and network protocols. Or the organization will need to extend those requirements specifically for the cloud, and in some cases, specifically for each service on the cloud, because each service is slightly different in how far it is from the hardware below.

The developers at regulated institutions, and those building software for organizations in regulated industries, are actually leveraging these managed services already, but commonly have little understanding and appreciation of the privacy, security, and compliance implications of using all of these different services that cloud providers offer. It's almost like "dark compliance" as a concept.

All of this clearly drives the need for a robust approach to compliance. It needs to be prescriptive at the highest level, while providing enough flexibility to adapt to any kind of policy, legislation, or regulatory change to which an industry must adhere, with GDPR being a perfect example.

The organizational compliance posture must be right at the highest-level to protect an organization, even as the whole relationship between compliance and the cloud is continually morphing and evolving. It all starts with compliance. Compliance should be the guiding light for any organization that consumes the cloud. The prescriptive compliance approach must map down to the highly dynamic cloud services environment in order to make the compliance hygiene of an organization actionable by IT, security, innovation, and any other groups within the organization that leverage the cloud.

The real challenge is found in mapping the prescriptive compliance approach and the policies down to the specifics, the application of that policy across the three major cloud providers and then from there, the fifty or one hundred, and possibly the multiple hundreds of managed and microservices in a few years. The list needs to be flexible and dynamic in mapping to new, emerging services and ensuring that they also map up to the prescriptive compliance regime. Using the gold standard of the past by creating relatively static run books or basic rules for configuration management no longer works in a cloud-first world.

This top down, highly dynamic approach to the cloud is referred to as *Complete Cloud Compliance*, or *3C* for short. A *3C* program is the new mandate for regulated companies because the cloud is creating new privacy and compliance challenges in every industry, in every geography on the planet. Layer in all the additional digital data being collected and leveraged for customer experiences, and the cloud becomes not just transformative, but high risk. Privacy and consumer advocacy groups are driving the conversation about new regulation and new requirements with compliance. These groups are rightfully concerned that consumers don't fully grasp what kind of data companies collect and what those companies do with that data. While conversations tend to focus on user privacy agreements and terms of service, regulations like GDPR, have real implications on business risk.

The content of this book focuses on compliance and the changes needed to succeed at de-risking the cloud for regulated industry organizations. The cloud is a new paradigm and *Complete Cloud Compliance* has the potential to dramatically reshape the way organizations perceive and operate in the cloud. It's time to embrace the change that has moved onto the doorstep of regulated industries.

Acknowledgements

The idea behind the book started with the encouragement of our friend Steven Gottlieb who heard what we had to say about this global challenge and pushed us to share it with those who need to hear it... We are thankful for team members Laleh Hassibi, Avtar Varma, and Matthew Taylor who collaborated on the content. Many other colleagues gave invaluable feedback throughout the process... Dr. Bryan Cline contributed feedback that helped both the accuracy and clarity of the content; his contributions are his own and do not necessarily reflect formal views from the HITRUST Alliance... The book was edited by long-time healthcare communications expert Marcia Noyes... Art direction came from John Zilly and his team at Milepost59. R. Allan White contributed to the design and created the final product.

About The Authors

Travis Good, MD

With a passion for healthcare and an eye towards market changing transformation, Travis blends his varied experience across medicine, cloud, and cybersecurity to develop impactful strategic initiatives. He has written extensively on healthcare technology and digital innovation and spoken at events like HIMSS, SXSW, AMIA, AHIMA, MedX, Health 2.0, and HITRUST Summit. As the co-founder and CEO of Datica, he created the strategy and go-to-market vision for products now helping enable innovation on the cloud at hundreds of healthcare organizations. Travis grew up in Florida before bouncing around for college and graduate school, eventually settling in Colorado with his family.

Kris Gösser

Kris likes to sit at the intersection of design, business, and technology to craft empathetic products for markets in need. He has been a Lean Startup practitioner across his twelve-year career as an entrepreneur spanning leadership roles in engineering, design, product, marketing, sales, and management. As the CMO of Datica, he interfaces with the healthcare industry to understand the challenges faced while guiding Datica's revenue machine towards growth targets. He helped write this book because he viewed a deeper understanding around the topic of cloud compliance as an essential ingredient to an improved society—the most regulated industries are often the most important to communities. A Wisconsin native, Kris and his family live in Seattle where they now call home.

KGOSSER@GMAIL.COM
262-358-0849

Endnotes

1   http://compliancecertification.org/Portals/2/PDF/CHC/ccb-chc-handbook.
    pdf

2   https://oig.hhs.gov/compliance/compliance-resource-portal/files/
    HCCA-OIG-Resource-Guide.pdf

3   https://en.wikipedia.org/wiki/Capability_Maturity_Model

4   https://www.us-cert.gov/bsi/articles/tools/modeling-tools/
    general-modeling-concept

5   https://www.hhs.gov/sites/default/files/ocr/privacy/hipaa/administrative/
    securityrule/techsafeguards.pdf

6   https://www.hhs.gov/sites/default/files/ocr/privacy/hipaa/administrative/
    securityrule/adminsafeguards.pdf

7   https://hitrustalliance.net/

8   https://hitrustalliance.net/understanding-leveraging-csf/

9   https://cloudsecurityalliance.org/star/#_overview

10 https://www.ca.com/content/dam/ca/us/files/ebook/insider-threat-report.
    pdf

11 https://healthitsecurity.com/news/
    stolen-computer-hard-drives-lead-to-health-data-breach-in-va

12 https://www.us-cert.gov/ncas/alerts/TA18-004A

13 https://www.hhs.gov/sites/default/files/april-2017-ocr-cyber-awareness-
    newsletter.pdf

14 https://nvlpubs.nist.gov/nistpubs/Legacy/SP/nistspecialpublication800-145.
    pdf

15 https://en.wikipedia.org/wiki/Edge_computing

16 https://aws.amazon.com/enterprise/hybrid/

17 https://cloud.google.com/gke-on-prem/

18 https://azure.microsoft.com/en-us/overview/azure-stack/

19 https://blogs.msdn.microsoft.com/azuresecurity/2016/04/18/
    what-does-shared-responsibility-in-the-cloud-mean/

20 https://datica.com/blog/inheritance-and-ownership-of-compliance-risk/

21 https://hitrustalliance.net/documents/mycsf/mycsf_information/
    CSFInheritanceDatasheet.pdf

22 https://dashboard.healthit.gov/evaluations/data-briefs/non-federal-acute-
    care-hospital-ehr-adoption-2008-2015.php

23 https://www.cms.gov/Outreach-and-Education/Look-Up-Topics/EHR-and-
    HITECH/EHR-HITECH-page.html

24 https://www.ncbi.nlm.nih.gov/pmc/articles/PMC3810528/

25 https://www.sciencedirect.com/science/article/pii/S0735675713004051

26 https://www.jwatch.org/fw111995/2016/09/06/
    half-physician-time-spent-ehrs-and-paperwork

27 https://www.healthcareitnews.com/news/hospital-it-spending-jumps-high

28 https://rockhealth.com/reports/2018-midyear-funding-review-digital-
    health-deja-vu-in-yet-another-record-breaking-half/

29 https://bvp.app.box.com/v/BVP-HealthcareValuescape

30 https://www.gartner.com/doc/3772081/hype-cycle-data-science-machine

31 https://www.zdnet.com/article/anatomy-of-the-target-data-breach-missed-
    opportunities-and-lessons-learned/

32 https://softwareengineeringdaily.com/tag/sam-ghods/

33 https://aws.amazon.com/compliance/hipaa-eligible-services-reference/

34 https://aws.amazon.com/fargate/

35 https://github.com/

36 https://about.gitlab.com/

37 https://www.nist.gov/publications/guide-conducting-risk-assessments

38 https://datica.com/blog/what-is-the-cost-of-a-hipaa-audit/

CPSIA information can be obtained
at www.ICGtesting.com
Printed in the USA
LVIC060945060119
602549LV00001BB/2